COMPUTE!'s
Quick & Easy
Guide to
PC *Excel*

John Adler

COMPUTE! Publications,Inc.**abc**

A Capital Cities/ABC, Inc. Company
Greensboro, North Carolina

Editor: Lynne Weatherman

Printed in the United States of America

10 9 8 7 6 5 4 3 2 1

ISBN 0-87455-140-4

COMPUTE! Publications, Inc., Post Office Box 5406, Greensboro, NC 27403, (919) 275-9809, is a Capital Cities/ABC, Inc. Company and is not associated with any manufacturer of personal computers. *Excel* is a trademark and Microsoft is a registered trademark of Microsoft Corporation. IBM PC is a registered trademark of International Business Machines.

Contents

Foreword

COMPUTE!'s Quick and Easy Guide to PC Excel will introduce
you to Excel, Microsoft's best-selling spreadsheet package for
the IBM PC. Among its multitude of powerful financial, database, and statistical features, Excel offers you the ability to link
data between worksheets, graph the data using one of the
many charts available, and easily create and run macros for
your more routine tasks.

However, with power comes complexity, and that's where
a fast, friendly guide like COMPUTE!'s Quick and Easy Guide to
PC Excel comes to your rescue.

Progressing in a logical format, this guide leads you from
the beginning steps of entering cell information through actually creating your own accounting, real estate, or database
models. Along the way you'll encounter power user tips and a
summary of Excel's commands.

And since it's from COMPUTE! Books, you know the
writing is clear, concise, and to the point. No need to wade
through hundreds of pages just to find the right keystroke.

So sit back and relax. With COMPUTE!'s Quick and Easy
Guide to PC Excel next to your PC, you'll be creating and
analyzing spreadsheet data faster than you ever thought
possible.

Introduction

Allow me to introduce you to *Excel,* the most powerful business program designed for a personal computer as of this writing. Originally designed for the Apple Macintosh, *Excel* has
been completely reworked and thoroughly embellished for the
lucky IBM owner who gets to use it. Without having lost any
of the user-friendliness Macintosh programs are known for,
the IBM version of *Excel* has a multitude of new features, allowing it to accommodate a wide range of sophistication
among its users. Anyone—from the first-time spreadsheet user
who merely wants a better way to balance a checkbook to the
computer software developer looking for a flexible programming language—will find *Excel* perfect for the task and eager
to serve.

The literature that comes with *Excel* can be quite over-
whelming. It is the purpose of this book to distill that material
into a useable, convenient form enabling you to get the most
from *Excel* with a minimal amount of reading.

Included in the introduction is information that discusses
the minimum hardware requirements needed to run *Excel.*
Also mentioned is specific hardware that can be purchased to
enhance the program.

Chapter 1 is a summary of all the commands accessed
from *Excel's* worksheet and chart menus. A concise explanation is given on how to use each command, followed by easy-
to-understand steps. Where appropriate, both the keyboard
command combination and the mouse reference are given.

Chapter 2 discusses the basics you need to know in order
to create an effective worksheet. Entering numbers, text, and
formulas into cells is explained.

Tips and techniques for the advanced user are discussed
in Chapter 3—specifically, how to get the most from macros,
functions, and arrays.

The last chapter gives general ideas on how to utilize *Excel* for business purposes. If you have used *Excel* before and
are in a hurry to try its applications, you may want to skip

right to this chapter. In addition to tips and techniques, short practical examples are given. Just follow the simple directions, and in a short time you'll be balancing your checkbook or amortizing your mortgage, to name a couple of examples. However, if you prefer to create your own customized worksheets, you are better off reading the entire book and familiarizing yourself with the program thoroughly.

The Command chart in Appendix A provides a quick reference which tells how to find and execute a command. It also features a list of the shortcut keys that correspond to the commands.

Appendix B describes the *Excel* functions available for your use. Appendix C contains instructions on how to convert data to and from other programs such as *dBase, Lotus 1-2-3,* and Microsoft's *Multiplan.*

Excel is a sophisticated business program that features spreadsheets, graphics, and databases. This combination makes it an invaluable tool that can save time and money for an individual or a business.

Below are some of the kinds of tasks and procedures you can perform with *Excel*.

Spreadsheets

With *Excel*'s worksheet (also known as a spreadsheet) you can create user-defined formats that allow you to customize your own models. They can assist you in accounting procedures, real estate computations, databases, and many other tasks. How to actually execute these models is demonstrated in the "Ideas" chapter, Chapter 4.

Accounting Procedures

It's possible to construct a working model to simplify many mundane accounting procedures. These models can be used for basic operating needs such as maintaining a checkbook, ledger, or other records such as cashflow and accounts receivable.

For instance, a normal checkbook can be replaced by a simple model that computes all credits and debits, maintains a running balance, and keeps a separate balance of all entries that have cleared the bank.

After you have completed a checkbook model, you can create a ledger worksheet to add on to it. A numerical code corresponding to an account number is added to each entry. This enables you to record and track discrete accounts for various categories such as rent, salaries, and supplies. These accounts are displayed to the right of the checkbook. With each entry you need only enter the appropriate code number and the program duplicates the entry in its correct account and adjusts the totals accordingly. A macro is then created to close out a current ledger and open a new one, transferring over any outstanding items and all previous closing balances.

Another model that can save a lot of time and frustration is a worksheet for projecting cashflow. You can create a worksheet template to cover any length of time you wish. For example, if you want to project cashflow over a three-month period, you enter expected total sales from three different profit centers over the next three months. The expected collection time is then entered by inputting the percentage of the first month's sales that will be received within 30 days and the percentage that will be received within 60 days. The 90-day percentage figure is then automatically calculated by finding the remainder.

Known receipts and disbursements are entered on the second section of the worksheet so that the running balance can be monitored. The worksheet takes the cash receipts from the first section and incorporates them into the schedule.

What-if projections can be made by inputting various percentages and sales figures on the first part of the worksheet and noting the effect they have on the running balance.

Another model can be created to track accounts receivable. You enter on the worksheet the date a payment is received, the date of the original invoice, and the amount collected. The program then computes how many days it takes to receive each payment and what percentage of receivables were paid in 30, 60, 90, and more than 90 days. This data can assist you in projecting cashflow by entering these percentages into the cashflow worksheet.

Real Estate Computations

Many intricate computations used in real estate can be calculated with much more ease on a customized worksheet.

With a present value worksheet you can determine the outstanding principal of a loan or figure out the status of the loan after any given number of payments. This is useful in determining how much it would cost to pay off a mortgage early. To compute the present value, you enter on the worksheet:

• The annual interest rate
• The term of the loan
• The payment per period
• The future value

The program then calculates and displays the present value.

You can also create a model to calculate future value. This is useful in determining a balloon payment or the value of a piece of property based on the rent and interest it yields. To compute the future value you enter on the worksheet:

• The interest rate
• The loan amount
• The term of the loan
• The payment per period

The future value is then calculated and displayed on the worksheet. You can also compute the status of the loan after any given number of payments with this model.

Another model can be created to determine the interest rate on a loan. You enter on the worksheet:

• The amount of the loan
• The term of the loan
• The payment per period
• The future value

The worksheet then calculates and displays the interest rate. As with the previous two worksheets, this one can compute the status of the loan after any given number of payments.

A loan amortization worksheet is an extremely beneficial real estate application. You can determine payment amount, how much of a given payment is principal, how much is interest, and the amount of remaining principal after any given payment. To do this, you enter:

- The interest rate
- The amount of the loan
- The term of the loan

Excel computes the total amount owed, as well as the total amount of interest paid over the life of the loan.

As you become more familiar with *Excel*, you'll discover that it has an almost limitless number of applications.

Databases

In addition to spreadsheets and graphics, *Excel* enables you to create databases. These are collections of information on the worksheet. They are organized as records, with each record divided into one or more fields. Each field represents a cell, the basic unit of a worksheet.

In these cells you can enter numbers, formulas, functions, and text. Once you have created a database using this information, you can easily find, sort, extract, or delete records.

Selection criteria enable you to use these functions to manipulate the information in the databases. Selection criteria are entries on a worksheet that are in a specifically defined area of cells—the criteria range.

There are two categories of criteria:

- Comparison criteria
- Computed criteria

Comparison criteria are used to extract information with like characteristics. For example, suppose you have a database made up of a list of names, ages, and incomes, and you want to locate the names of everyone who makes $50,000 per year. Rather than go through each record manually, you could direct the program to get the information for you, using the criteria range.

The criteria you select does not have to be an exact match. For instance, in the previous example you could direct the program to locate the names of everyone who makes more than $50,000 yearly.

You can also combine criteria. For instance, you can locate the names of everyone under 35 whose annual salary is also more than $50,000. You can even go a step further, and direct the program to get the names of everyone *between* the ages of 30 and 35 whose annual salary is more than $50,000.

Computed criteria are more complex, enabling you to use a formula to locate needed information. For instance, you can use a computed criterion to find records in which the income entry divided by the age entry produces a value greater than a specified number.

Computed criteria can also be used to compare entries. For example, you can use these criteria to select every record in an employee database in which the length of employment entry is two years more than the one above it.

We have discussed the fundamentals of databases. More information on databases will be offered in later chapters.

Charts

With *Excel*'s versatile graphics display, any concept stemming from a set of figures can be illustrated and clarified. This program enables you to create sophisticated, quality graphs to augment or replace worksheets. You can select from six types:

- Area charts
- Bar charts
- Column charts
- Line graphs
- Pie charts
- Scatter diagrams

Commands used to create charts are described in Chapter 1, the "Command Summary."

System Requirements

A few basic requirements are necessary before you can use the *Excel* program. First of all, you will need a system that meets these requirements:

IBM Personal System/2, IBM PC AT, Compaq Deskpro 386, or 100-percent compatible
IBM VGA, IBM EGA, or IBM EGA Hi-Res Monitor
640K memory
DOS 3.0 or higher
Hard disk

Optionally, you can use:

Microsoft Mouse
8087, 80287, 80387 math coprocessor
Network system compatible with Microsoft Networks

Excel works very smoothly with a mouse—in fact, the original program for the Apple Macintosh was designed to run with a mouse first, and with a keyboard second. The IBM version of *Excel* has given more emphasis to the keyboard, but the program can be most quickly learned and most easily used with a mouse.

Printing. For printing documents, *Excel* is supplied with drivers for most popular printers, and more drivers are on the way. More than one printer can be installed so that a choice of printers can be made at printout time.

Extended and expanded memory. *Excel* makes good use of extended memory, and even better use of expanded memory. *Excel* is supplied with a utility program, SMARTDRV.SYS, which utilizes extended or expanded memory by making a disk cache, allowing the program to run faster and access the hard drive less.

Expanded memory is sensed by *Excel* and automatically utilized. It allows you to have more applications open at once under Windows, and allows *Excel* to run faster and hold larger worksheets.

Installing and Starting *Excel*

When you are ready to use *Excel:*

- Place the Setup disk in Drive A
- From your hard drive (C:) type
  A: To change to Drive A; then type
  setup to start the Setup program

   Follow the directions in the program. (Setup allows you to tell Excel what kind of monitor and printer you are using, along with a good deal of other information.)

   When Setup has finished and you want to start *Excel,* change to the drive and directory where *Excel* is installed and:

- Type **EXCEL**
- Press Enter

Chapter 1
Command Summary

Chapter 1
Command Summary

In order to make use of *Excel*'s many features you must know *Excel*'s commands. This chapter lists all of the commands and describes how they work.

Excel gives you more than one way to execute a command. Besides using the mouse or keyboard directional keys to display and choose a command from a menu, you are sometimes able to use a *keyboard equivalent*. A keyboard equivalent is a combination of keys which, when pressed, executes a command in exactly the same way that using the mouse to choose the command from the menu does.

After the command (where appropriate) is listed its keyboard equivalent, and in some cases, even a *keyboard equivalent shortcut*. If the keys listed are separated by hyphens (Alt-R-E), that means to press the first key, release it, then press the next key, release it, and so forth. If the keys are separated by plus signs (Alt + R + E), press them simultaneously.

Worksheet Menus

When you first start the program, *Excel* automatically displays a new worksheet. At the top of the worksheet is the menu bar, which lists the ten worksheet command menus: Control, File, Edit, Formula, Format, Data, Options, Macro, Window, and Help.

Full and Short menus. In *Excel* you have a choice of working with either Full or Short menus. In Short menus, the most commonly used commands are listed. In Full menus, all the Short menus commands are listed, plus the more advanced and specialized ones. You will probably want to work in Full menus for now, and change to Short menus when you are more familiar with the *Excel* program.

To use Full menus:
• Choose Full menus from the Options menu.

3

Figure 1-1. The Menu Bar

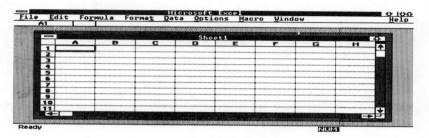

To use Short menus:
• Choose Short menus from the Options menu.

To select a menu using the keyboard:
• Press Alt and release.
• Press the underlined letter on the menu you want.
    (To select the Control menu, press the Alt key and then
the space bar.)
Or
• Press Alt and release.
• Press the directional cursor keys until the menu you want is
highlighted.
• Press Enter.

To select a menu using the mouse:
• Point to the menu you want.
• Click the mouse button. The menu you select appears with a
list of commands.

To select a command once the menu is displayed:
• Press the appropriate underlined letter.
Or
• Point to the command you want and click the mouse button.
Or
• Press the cursor-up and -down keys until the command you
want is highlighted.
• Press Enter.

Pressing Escape always allows you to get out of a menu.
Only those commands that are applicable to the status of your
worksheet may be selected. These will be displayed in black

(or reverse video). The gray options are those that are currently of no use to you, and are not available.

To choose the OK button in a dialog box you can either click it with your mouse or press Enter. There's more about using the keyboard and mouse, choosing dialog box buttons, and using special function keys in Chapter 2, "How to Use *Excel*."

Control Menu

Figure 1-2. The Control Menus

Restore	Alt+F5
Move	Alt+F7
Size	Alt+F8
Mi_n_imize	Alt+F9
Ma_x_imize	Alt+F10
_C_lose	Alt+F4
R_u_n . . .	

Restore	Ctrl+F5
Move	Ctrl+F7
Size	Ctrl+F8
Maximize	Ctrl+F10
_C_lose	Ctrl+F4
Split	

There are two Control menus available for your use. One controls the application window and the other controls the document window. A particular window's Control menu is also located at the upper left corner of the window and is represented by the Control menu icon. (In the application window this icon is a space bar; in the document window it is a hyphen.) These menus are common to all Windows applications, and control the status of the windows. Note that some commands are not on both menus.

Restore Command
♦ Alt–Space bar–R (application)
♦ Alt-Minus-R (document)
Or
♦ Alt + F5 (application)
♦ Ctrl + F5 (document)

If a window has been Minimized or Maximized, this command restores it to its previous size. Otherwise, the command is grayed, indicating it is invalid. If the window to be restored displays a pair of arrows in the upper right-hand corner, it can be restored with the mouse by clicking on those arrows.

To use the Restore command:
• Choose Restore from the Control menu.

Move Command
♦ Alt–Space bar–M (application)
♦ Alt-Minus-M (document)
Or
♦ Alt + F7 (application)
♦ Ctrl + F7 (document)

Move lets you move a window to a different location on the screen. This command does not affect the window's size.

To use the Move command:
• Choose it from the Control menu.
• Use the directional cursor keys to move the window. Hold down the Control key while using the direction keys to make the window move more slowly.
• After the window is positioned where you want it, press Enter.

If you have a mouse, you can also move the window by pointing to the window's title bar and dragging. A Maximized window cannot be moved.

Size Command
♦ Alt–Space bar–S (application)
♦ Alt-Minus-S (document)

Or
- Alt + F8 (application)
- Ctrl + F8 (document)

This command lets you change the size of a window, assuming it is not Maximized or Minimized.

To use the Size command:
- Choose it from the Control menu.
- Use the directional cursor keys to adjust the size of the window. Hold down the Control key while using the direction keys to make the window move more slowly.
- After the window is sized correctly, press Enter.

If you have a mouse, you can also size the window by pointing to the gray window border and dragging. Pointing to a corner allows you to change both the horizontal and vertical dimensions simultaneously.

Minimize Command
- Alt-Spacebar-N
Or
- Alt + F9

This command reduces the Excel window to a small icon at the bottom of your screen.

To use the Minimize command:
- Choose it from the Control menu.

Maximize Command
- Alt–Space bar–X (application)
- Alt-Minus-X (document)
Or
- Alt + F10 (application)
- Ctrl + F10 (document)

This command enlarges a window to its maximum size within the available space.

When used on the *Excel* window, *Excel* occupies the entire screen. When used on a document window, the document occupies the entire *Excel* window.

To use the Maximize command:
• Choose it from the Control menu.

A window can also be Maximized with the mouse by pointing to the up-arrow symbol in the upper right-hand corner of the window and clicking. To restore a window to its previous size, choose the Restore command.

Close Command
♦ Alt–Space bar–C (application)
♦ Alt-Minus-C (document)
Or
♦ Alt + F4 (application)
♦ Ctrl + F4 (document)

Choose this command to close a window.

If you choose this command, but have not saved the changes to your document, a dialog box prompts you to save the changes before the window is closed.

If you choose to close the *Excel* application window, this ends the *Excel* session. Again, you'll be given an opportunity to save document changes that have not yet been written to disk. Some dialog boxes also have Control menus, and can be closed using this command.

To use the Close command:
• Choose it from the Control menu.

Split Command
♦ Alt-Minus-T

This command lets you split a window into *panes* so that different sections of a worksheet can be viewed simultaneously. It only appears on worksheet and macro window menus.

The difference between this command and the New Window command on the Windows menu is that this command allows simultaneous scrolling, since the two panes are locked together.

To use the Split command:
- Choose it from the Control menu.
- Gray lines appear that cross at the upper left corner of the worksheet.
- Use the direction keys to move the bars to the location where the window should be split.
- Press Enter.

Or, use your mouse to choose Control Split and then move the split panes pointer until the bars are at the correct location; then click.

Run Command
♦ Alt–Space bar–U

This command lets you run the Clipboard, Control Panel, and Macro Translation Assistant.

To use it:
- Choose Run from the Control menu.
- Choose which of the applications you want to run from the dialog box that appears:
    Clipboard shows the Clipboard contents.
    Control Panel allows you to add or delete printer drivers, fonts, and communication ports, and change your mouse buttons and screen colors.
    Macro Translator converts *Lotus 1-2-3* macros to *Excel* macros.
- Choose OK.

File Menu

The File menu consists of commands used to create new documents and to retrieve, save, delete, and print existing ones.

Figure 1-3. The File Menu

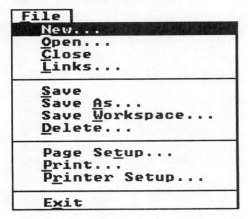

New Command

Figure 1-4. The New Dialog Box

◆ Alt-F-N

Or

◆ Alt + F1(chart)
   Alt + Shift + F1 (worksheet)
   Alt + Ctrl + F1 (macro)

   To create a new file:
• Choose the New command from the File menu.

   A dialog box like the one shown in Figure 1-4 appears. Choose the option for the kind of document you want to create—worksheet, chart, or macro sheet.

- Choose OK. (Or you can simply double-click the option you want.)

Open Command
- Alt-F-O

Or

- Alt + Ctrl + F2

To retrieve an existing document for editing, use the Open command:
- Choose the Open command from the File menu.
- A dialog box containing an alphabetical list of documents on the disk drive and subdirectory you are using appears. You may select one of these, or type in a filename in the text box.

Files from other acceptable formats, such as *Lotus 1-2-3*, *Multiplan*, and *dBase*, will not be listed, but can be opened by typing in the name of the file you want.

If you want to access a document on another disk drive or subdirectory, choose it from the list, or choose .. to go to the next highest subdirectory.

Figure 1-5. The Open Dialog Box

- When the file you want to open is selected (or entered in the text box) choose OK.

Links Command (Full Menus)
- Alt-F-L

Documents that are linked to the one you are working on can be opened with the Links command. This command displays a list of supporting worksheets and an Open and Cancel button.

11

To use the Links command:
• Choose it from the File menu.
• A dialog box containing a list of supporting worksheets appears. You can make as many selections as you want: If the documents you need are listed consecutively, hold down the shift key while using a direction key; if they are not listed consecutively, use the Control key along with the direction key and space bar.
• After you have selected the documents you want to open, choose OK. If you are merely viewing supporting worksheets and don't wish to open them, choose the Cancel button.

If the current directory does not contain any supporting worksheets, the files are listed with a full pathname. If they are opened and later saved, they will be saved to their original directory.

The Change option allows you to switch the references on the active worksheet to another worksheet. You simply select or type in the name of the new worksheet, and *Excel* updates all of the references. Cell references remain the same—only worksheet references change.

The Read-Only box lets you open a document, but not change it. This is useful in preventing inadvertent changes, and in allowing others on a network to have access to the same document. Only one network user at a time has write privileges to a particular document.

Save Command
♦ Alt-F-S
Or
♦ Alt + Shift + F2

Use the Save Command to save a previously named document. (To save and name a document for the first time use the Save As command.) The document you are saving will not be closed, but will remain on the screen. If you have not yet named the document, you'll be given an opportunity to do so in a dialog box.

To save changes to a document:
- Select an active window containing the changes you wish to save.
- Choose Save from the File menu.

It is a good idea to do this periodically, even if you have not finished working with the document. This precludes the loss of all of your work in the event of a power failure.

Save As Command

Figure 1-6. Save As Dialog Box

```
┌─────────────────────────────────────────────────────┐
│  Save Worksheet as:        (        Ok        )      │
│  [SHEET1.XLS          ]    (     Cancel      )       │
│  C:\XL                     (  Options  >> )          │
│  ┌─File Format──────────────────────────────┐        │
│  │ ⊙ Normal      ○ SYLK        ○ DIF        │        │
│  │ ○ Text        ○ WKS         ○ DBF 2      │        │
│  │ ○ CSV         ○ WK1         ○ DBF 3      │        │
│  └──────────────────────────────────────────┘        │
│  Password: [                              ]          │
│  □ Create Backup File                               │
└─────────────────────────────────────────────────────┘
```

- Alt-F-A

Or

- Alt + F2

The Save As command is used to save and name a document for the first time, or to save a new version of an existing document by giving it a new name.

To use the Save As command:
- Select the document you want to save.
- Choose Save As from the File menu.
- Type a name for the document in the dialog box that appears.
- Choose OK.

13

If the file has been named already, that name will be proposed. You may accept it or change it in order to preserve the existing version under the old name.

If the name you type already exists on the disk, you'll be asked if you want to replace the document with the new one. If you wish to replace the old one, choose OK; otherwise choose Cancel.

To save the document to another drive or subdirectory, type in the full pathname before the name of the file.

Choose Options to save the document in another format, preserve a backup copy of the document, or make access to the document available only by password.

Save Workspace Command (Full Menus)

Figure 1-7. The Save Workspace Dialog Box

```
Save Workspace as:        [    OK    ]
[FINANCE.XLW              ]  [ Cancel ]
C:\XL
```

♦ Alt-F-W

To save all open documents, choose this command. *Excel* creates a new file with the name of your choice and the extension XLW. In this file is a list of all the documents which were open at the time Save Workspace was used.

To use this command:
• Choose Save Workspace from the File menu.
• A dialog box appears in which you type the name of your workspace file. In this workspace file are saved the names of the documents open (worksheets, macro sheets, charts, and so on) when you chose the command.
• Choose OK.

Choosing this workspace filename when using the Open command causes all documents listed in the file to be opened simultaneously.

The workspace file does *not* contain the actual documents, but only a *list* of the documents. Do not delete documents assuming they are in the workspace (XLW) file.

Using Save Workspace effects a save on all documents changed since the last Save Workspace command. This is a handy command to use before exiting *Excel*.

Delete Command (Full Menus)
♦ Alt-F-D

To delete documents from the current drive/directory:
• Choose the Delete command from the File menu.
• A dialog box appears with a list of all documents and applications on the disk. That list can be narrowed down by typing in a file specifier. For example, if you only want to see worksheet files, type *.XLS. You may change directories by choosing one from the Directories box.

Figure 1-8. The Delete Dialog Box

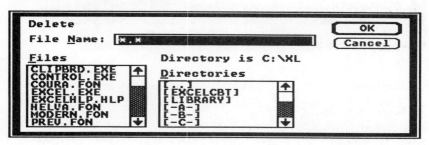

• Use the cursor keys or mouse to select the document you want to delete.
• Choose OK.

After you have deleted a document it is removed from the disk permanently and cannot be retrieved. However, if you inadvertently delete a document that is still displayed on the screen, you can use the Save As command to save it onto the disk.

Page Setup Command
♦ Alt-F-T

You can control the appearance of the printed document with the Page Setup command. This command makes it possible to produce professional-looking reports.

To use this command:
• Choose Page Setup from the File menu.
• Enter the appropriate options in the dialog box that appears.

Figure 1-9. The Page Setup Dialog Box

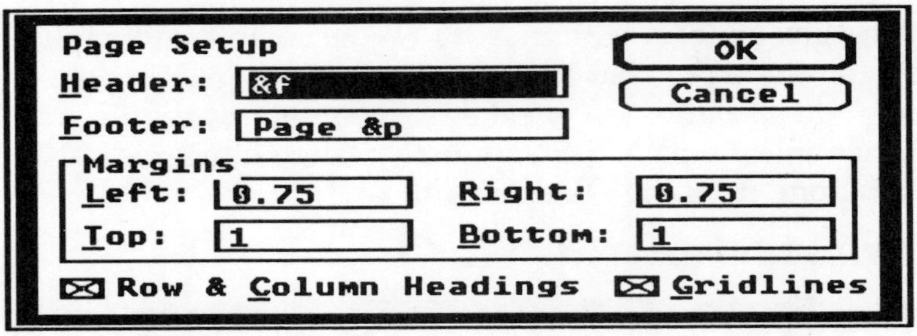

```
┌─────────────────────────────────────────────────────┐
│                                                      │
│  Page Setup                    ┌──────────────┐      │
│  Header: [&f          ]        │     OK       │      │
│  Footer: [ Page &p    ]        └──────────────┘      │
│  ┌Margins────────────┐         ┌──────────────┐      │
│  │Left: [0.75  ]   Right: [0.75 ] │ Cancel  │        │
│  │Top:  [1     ]   Bottom: [1   ]                     │
│                                                      │
│  ⊠ Row & Column Headings   ⊠ Gridlines               │
└─────────────────────────────────────────────────────┘
```

• Choose OK.

The alignment and contents of the header and footer can be specified. By default, *Excel* fills in the document name as the header and the page number as the footer. Certain codes, indicated by an ampersand (&), specify certain printing instructions. The chart below shows the available commands and their meanings.

Command	Meaning
&&	Print a single ampersand.
&B	Print the left, center, or right part of the header or footer in bold.
&C	Center the characters that follow.
&D	Print the current date.
&F	Print the name of the document.
&I	Print the left, center, or right part of the header or footer in italic.
&L	Left-align the characters that follow.
&P	Print the page number.
&P + *number*	Add *number* to the page number and print it. (Use to change the starting page number.)

&P — *number*   Subtract *number* from the page number and print it.
&R   Right-align the characters that follow.
&T   Print the current time.

These commands can be used for headers or footers, and can be combined. For example, &LProfits&C&D&R&T would left-align the word *Profits,* center the date, and right-align the time.

The margins can be specified. The units are inches if *Excel* was installed for a U.S. keyboard. You can choose to print or omit the row/column headings and gridlines.

If a chart is active, certain other options appear. You may choose to print the chart the same size as the screen (pick Screen Size), to fill the page while retaining the aspect ratio appearing on the screen (pick Fit to Page), or to fill up the page regardless of the aspect ratio (pick Full Page).

Print Command
♦ Alt-F-P
Or
♦ Ctrl + Shift + F2
♦ Crtl + Shift + F12

The Print command lets you print an entire worksheet or just a portion of one.

To print the entire document:
• Choose Print from the File menu.
• Select from the available options.
• Choose OK.

To print only a portion of a worksheet:
• Select the range of cells you wish to print.
• Choose Set Print Area from the Options Menu.
• Choose Print from the File menu.
• Choose OK.

You may preview the printout by selecting Preview. You'll be shown a layout of the entire page and given the following options:

Command	Meaning
Cancel	Cancels command and returns you to document.
Next	Displays next page of the printed document.
Previous	Displays previous page of printed document.
Print	Uses the option set in the File Print dialog box to print document.
Zoom	Expands page to display it full-size; you can then scroll to different parts of your document for viewing. Choosing Zoom again returns your document to preview size.

Draft quality prints the document using the printer's own characters rather than the graphically defined *Excel* characters. The quality is not as good, but it prints a lot faster.

If you have entered notes using that option from the Formula menu, you may print them out by selecting Notes or Both, which prints out the worksheet and the notes.

Printer Setup Command
♦ Alt-F-R

The Printer Setup Command tells the program what type of printer you are using. You may choose among all of the printers that have been installed.

To choose a different printer from the one you are using:
• Choose Printer Setup from the File menu.
• Select the printer you want from the list in the dialog box that appears.
• Choose OK.
• Choose the Run command from the Control menu (Alt–Space bar–U).

Choosing Setup from the Printer Setup dialog box displays information about the printer selected in the dialog box.

Record Command
♦ Alt-F-C

Choosing this command enables all keystrokes to be recorded so that they can be repeated later by running a macro. This option usually appears on the Macro menu, but appears here when all documents are either closed or hidden.

Unhide Window Command
♦ Alt-F-U

This command shows windows which are hidden. It usually appears on the Windows menu, but appears here when there are no open or unhidden windows.

To use this command:
• Choose Unhide Window from the File menu.
• Select the window you want to unhide from the dialog box that appears.
• Choose OK.

If you have used the Options Protect Document command to protect the window, you must supply the window's password before the window will be unhidden.

Exit Command
♦ Alt-F-X

To close the program and all opened documents, choose the Exit command.

To use this command:
• Choose Exit from the File menu.
• A dialog box appears and asks whether you want to save the changes in any documents that have been changed since last saved.
• Choose Yes to save the changes to that document, choose No to ignore the changes to the document, or choose Cancel to cancel the Exit command and return to the document you were working on.

If a copied selection is outlined by a marquee, it will be saved to the Clipboard when you exit, making it available to transfer into other Windows applications.

Edit Menu

Figure 1-10. The Edit Menu

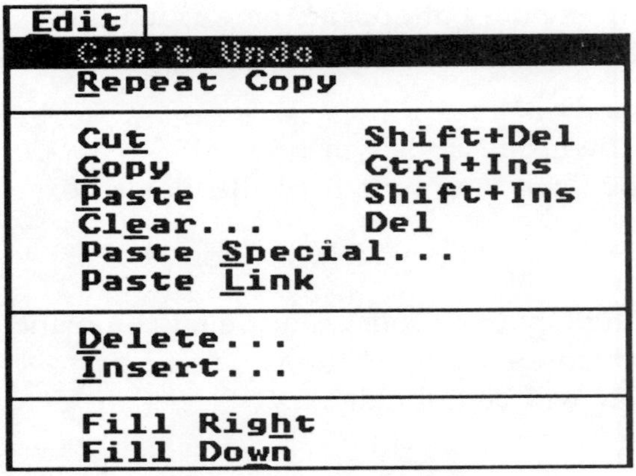

```
┌─────────┐
│ Edit    │
├─────────┴────────────────────────┐
│  Can't Undo                      │
│  Repeat Copy                     │
├──────────────────────────────────┤
│  Cut            Shift+Del        │
│  Copy           Ctrl+Ins         │
│  Paste          Shift+Ins        │
│  Clear...       Del              │
│  Paste Special...                │
│  Paste Link                      │
├──────────────────────────────────┤
│  Delete...                       │
│  Insert...                       │
├──────────────────────────────────┤
│  Fill Right                      │
│  Fill Down                       │
└──────────────────────────────────┘
```

Edit menu commands let you make timesaving maneuvers and instantaneous corrections.

Undo/Can't Undo Command
♦ Alt-E-U

The Undo command lets you reverse commands from the Edit menu, undo typing in the formula bar, and undo formula or values entered on the worksheet.

You can only undo a command before selecting another one. That is, as long as you do not make another entry or choose another command, you can undo a command.

The Undo command displays a command name to reflect your last Edit command. For example, if you use the Clear command to erase something and then realize you need to retrieve it, you can correct the mistake by choosing Undo Clear from the Edit menu.

If you are editing an entry in the formula bar and make an error, you can choose Undo Typing to restore the original entry.

Undo *cannot* be used on:
- File Delete
- Data Delete
- Data Extract

To use this command:
- Choose Undo from the Edit menu or press Alt-E-U.

Repeat Command (Full Menus)
♦ Alt + Enter

This command repeats the last command you chose, including any changed options in a dialog box. The Repeat command does not work on all commands, but is helpful for actions such as applying a font or format change to more than one group of cells.

Cut, Copy, Paste Commands
♦ Alt-E-T *or* ♦ Shift + Delete   Cut
♦ Alt-E-C *or* ♦ Ctrl + Insert   Copy
♦ Alt-E-P *or* ♦ Shift + Insert   Paste

The Cut command works in conjunction with the Copy and Paste commands. These three commands essentially act as scissors, eraser, and paste, and can save you a great deal of time when you're constructing a worksheet.

The Cut and Paste commands enable you to move a cell or range of cells to another area of your worksheet. You simply select an area to *cut* and then *paste* it in another selected area. The area you select must be rectangular and must be a continuous range of cells.

You may also use the Cut command when the formula bar is active. In this case the material selected in the formula bar is copied to the Clipboard, replacing its contents. It can then be pasted onto the formula bar at the insertion point.

To cut and paste in four easy steps:
- First, select the cells you wish to move. (Keep in mind that once you cut these cells, the program automatically deletes their contents.)

• Next, click the Cut command from the Edit menu. This puts a dotted line (marquee) around the entries you have selected.
• Select the cells to which you want to move the information. This area size must correspond to or exceed that of the original cells.
• Choose the Paste command from the Edit menu. Any existing data will be replaced with the information you wish to paste.

After you have cut and pasted, *Excel* automatically adjusts any formulas on the worksheet that refer to the moved cells to make sure that they refer to the new location.

With the *Excel* Cut and Paste commands you can only specify one paste area. If you need to transfer the contents of a cell to more than one area, you need to use the Copy command.

The Copy and Paste commands let you duplicate the cell range onto other designated areas of the worksheet without eliminating the information of the original cell. Copy can be used on the formula bar and on entire charts, as well. If another application is selected after the Copy command, the material is placed on the Clipboard for transfer to another Windows application.

To use the Copy and Paste commands:
• Begin by selecting the area you wish to duplicate.
• Choose Copy from the Edit menu.
• Select the area where you want the copies to be placed.
• Choose Paste from the Edit menu.

With these commands you can select as many paste areas as you like without disturbing the original cell content.

The Copy command, unlike the Cut and Paste command, allows you to designate multiple, discontinuous paste areas. For example, it is possible to copy the contents of a single cell into three cells that are located in separate columns of the worksheet.

To Copy to multiple, discontinuous paste areas:
• Select the cell you wish to copy.
• Choose the Copy command.

- Select the first cell to which you wish to paste, hold down the Control key, and select the next two cells to which you wish to paste.

    To copy ranges:
- Select the cells you wish to copy.
- Choose the Copy command from the Edit menu. A marquee will appear around the designated range.
- Select the area to which you wish to paste. If the area is a continuous range, you need not select all the cells in the area. Simply select the cell in the upper left corner of the range.

Copy Picture Command
- Alt-Shift + E-C

Copy Picture copies your current selection to the Clipboard, where you can move it into another application—such as a word processor. This makes it easy to move sections of your worksheet or chart into reports or documents you are creating.

    This command is on the Edit menu only if you press the shift key while selecting the Edit menu.

Clear Command
- Alt-E-E
Or
- Del

With the Clear command you can clear a cell's formula, format, notes, or any combination.

    To clear a cell:
- Select the cell or range of cells you want to clear.
- Choose Clear from the Edit menu. A dialog box appears with the options: All, Formats, Formulas, Notes. Choose the appropriate selections.

Figure 1-11. The Clear Dialog Box

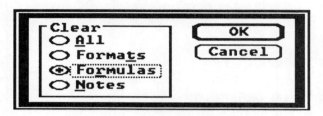

• Choose OK.

You can also clear formulas and values by pressing the Delete key, thus bypassing the menu and dialog box.

The Clear command can be used on the formula bar as well, but there it operates a little differently. In that case it clears only the selected characters.

You can retrieve cleared cells by using the Undo command if you have not already used another command.

Clearing a cell merely removes the cell's contents; it doesn't delete the cell. Thus, if other cells have formulas containing a reference to a cleared cell, they may produce inaccurate results, as *Excel* will assume a value of 0 for the cleared cell. Therefore, it is very important to remove cells and close up space with the Delete command. Then if another cell has a formula containing a reference to the deleted cell, the program will display the #*REF!* error value rather than erroneously calculate results of the formula.

Paste Special Command (Full Menus)
♦ Alt-E-S
Or
♦ Shift + Insert

Paste Special is used in conjunction with the Copy command when you want to copy only a portion of a cell. Paste Special enables you to copy only the formulas, only the values, only the formats, only the notes, or any combination of the four.

To use the Paste Special command:
• Select the cell or cell range you wish to use.
• Choose the Copy command.

Command
Summary

- Select the paste area.
- Choose the Paste Special command. This produces a Paste Special dialog box. You can then specify the portion of the cell you wish to copy by selecting from the following options: All, Formulas, Values, Formats, Notes.

     Then select from the operation options:
  - *None* replaces cells in the paste area with cells from the copy area.
  - *Add* adds specified parts from the copy area to cells in the paste area.
  - *Subtract* subtracts the designated portions of the copy area cells from the paste area cells.
  - *Multiply* multiplies the specifed contents of the two ranges.
  - *Divide* divides the specifed contents of the paste area cells by the copy area cells.
- After you have selected an operation option, press Enter or Escape to cancel.

     Paste Special can also be used on a chart. You can specify the data series of the chart by copying it from the worksheet.

Paste Link Command (Full Menus)

This command allows you to paste copied data into your current selection and create a link between the source of the copied data and your current worksheet. If you change the source data, your worksheet is automatically updated to reflect those changes. Your source data can come from the same worksheet, another Excel worksheet, or another application.

     To use this command:
- Copy the source data.
- Select the cell or range where you want to paste the data.
- Choose Edit Paste Link.

Delete Command

- Alt-E-D

Or

- Ctrl + Minus

     Rather than just clearing a cell's content and leaving the empty cell on the worksheet, the Delete command removes cells, rows, and columns entirely. You can then close up the space remaining between the cells.

To delete cells and close up space:
• Select the area you want to delete.
• Choose the Delete command.
• A dialog box appears from which you can choose the Shift Cells Left option (which shifts the remaining cells to the left), or the Shift Cells Up option (which shifts the remaining cells up). Simply select the option you want; then choose OK or Cancel.

Figure 1-12. The Delete Dialog Box (Edit Menu)

Insert Command
♦ Alt-E-I
Or
♦ Crtl + Plus

Use the Insert command to add blank cells, rows, or columns between other cells on a worksheet.

To use this command:
• Simply select the area in which you wish to insert blank cells.
• Choose the Insert command from the Edit menu.
• A dialog appears giving you the option to Shift Cells Right (which shifts the selection to the right when the cells are inserted), or Shift Cells Down (which shifts the remaining cells down). Choose the option you want and then choose OK or Cancel.

If you are inserting entire rows or columns, no dialog box appears.

Figure 1-13. The Insert Dialog Box

Fill Right, Fill Down Commands

- Alt-E-H *or* ◆ Ctrl + >   Fill Right
- Alt-E-W *or* ◆ Crtl + <   Fill Down

In some instances it is possible, and easier, to use the Fill Right and Fill Down commands rather than the Copy and Paste commands. These commands can be used when you need to copy one or more cells into an adjacent set of cells.

Fill Right copies the data in the leftmost cells of the range into the rest of the cells in the range. Fill Down copies the data in the top cells of a range into the rest of the cells in the range. The results of these commands are identical to those of the Copy and Paste commands. Any existing entries in the fill area are replaced with the transferred data, just as with the Copy command.

To use the Fill Right or Fill Down command:
- Select the cells you want to copy and the cells you wish to fill.
- Choose Fill Right in order to copy the first column of cells you designated to the right.
Or
- Choose Fill Down to copy the first row of selected cells down.

Any formulas or values in the cells to which you are copying are replaced with those of the first row or column. It's important to be aware of whether cell references mentioned in formulas are relative or absolute, since the two produce entirely different results when you're copying cells. (See below for an explanation of the Reference command on the Formula menu).

It's also possible to Fill Up and Fill Left by holding down the shift key when you're choosing the Edit menu. These choices then replace the others.

Formula Menu

Creating complex formulas and naming cells are processes that can be simplified with commands from the Formula menu.

Figure 1-14. The Formula Menu

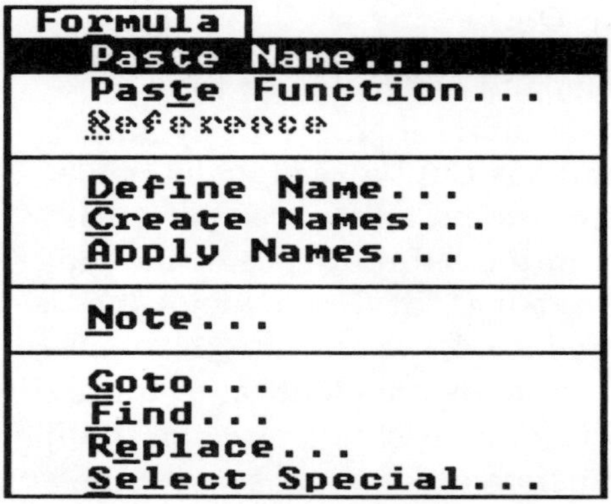

```
┌─────────────┐
│ Formula     │
│   Paste Name...
│   Paste Function...
│   Reference
├─────────────
│   Define Name...
│   Create Names...
│   Apply Names...
├─────────────
│   Note...
├─────────────
│   Goto...
│   Find...
│   Replace...
│   Select Special...
└─────────────
```

Paste Name Command
♦ Alt-R-P
Or
♦ F3

Just below the menu bar on the worksheet is the formula bar. With the Paste Name command you can enter names in this area.

To use the Paste Name command:
• Activate the formula bar by pressing F2 or pointing to the cursor with the mouse and clicking.
• Select an insertion point with the direction keys or with the mouse.
• Choose Paste Name from the formula menu.
• A dialog box appears with a list of the names you entered—with the Define Name or Create Name commands—for the

worksheet you are currently using. (These commands are explained below.) Select a name from this list.
• Choose OK.

Figure 1-15. Paste Name Dialog Box

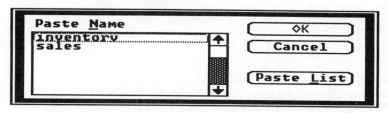

If Paste Name is selected when the formula bar is not active, *Excel* activates it and pastes the name into it. Otherwise it
pastes the name at the insertion point.

If no names have been defined, the Paste Name command
will dim. Before using it you will then need to define names
with the Define Name or Create Names command.

Names defined on another worksheet can be entered into
the formula bar of the active worksheet. Simply type the name
of the worksheet you are referring to; then type an exclama-
tion point, followed by the name defined on that worksheet.
For example, if you want to refer to the name *Salaries* on the
Employee worksheet, you type *Employees!Salaries*.

If you choose Paste List in the Paste Name dialog box, a
list of names and what they refer to is pasted on your document, starting at the active cell. This list replaces anything already in the cells, so be sure that the active cell is in a blank
area before you select Paste List.

Paste Function Command
♦ Alt-R-T
Or
♦ Shift + F3

Functions can be entered into the formula bar with the Paste
Function command.

To paste a function:
- Choose an insertion point in the formula bar.
- Click the Paste Function.
- A box appears containing a list of all available functions. Scroll through the list and select the function you wish to use.
- Choose OK.

Figure 1-16. Paste Function Box

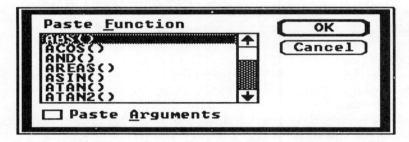

Paste Arguments is an option which pastes text descriptions of the necessary function arguments along with the functions. You then go back and replace these argument labels with actual arguments. If a function has more than one form, the various forms appear in another box and you select one.

You can type a function directly into a formula, thus bypassing this command, although mistakes can creep in more easily that way.

Reference Command
- Alt-R-R

Or

- F4

With the Reference command, selected references in a formula can be converted from relative to absolute, absolute to mixed, or mixed to relative.

A relative reference gives *Excel* directions on how to get to a designated cell from the cell with the formula in it. For example, if you enter the number 10 into cell A1, the number 20

into cell C1, and the formula =A1 into cell A3, you are direct-
ing the program to move up two cells, get the value of that
cell, and display it in the cell with the formula. Cell A3 then
displays the value 10.

    If you next copy the formula in cell A3 and paste it into
cell C3, the program goes up two cells and gets the value from
C1, then enters 20 in C3.

    An absolute reference, on the other hand, always refers to
the same cell, regardless of where the formula is moved. If an
absolute reference were used in the above formula, =A1
would be changed to $A$1, indicating that both column and
row are absolute. Cell C3 would then refer to cell A1 and display a 10, despite the transfer of the formula.

    With mixed references you can designate only the column
or only the row as absolute, and make the other relative.

    To change a reference:
- Select the one you wish to change in the formula bar.
- Choose the Reference command.

Define Name Command
- Alt-R-D

Or
- Ctrl + F3

To create a name for a cell, value, or formula, use the Define
Name command. This command also enables you to edit or
delete names.

    The first character of the name must be a letter. Subse-
quent characters, however, can be letters, digits, periods, or
underlines. The name cannot exceed 255 characters and may
not contain any spaces. To indicate a space, use ( ). *Excel* will
not accept any names that resemble absolute or relative
references.

    To define a name:
- Select the cell or range of cells you wish to name.
- Choose the Define Name command.
- A dialog box appears with a List box and a Name box as
  shown in Figure 1-17.

Figure 1-17. The Define Name Dialog Box

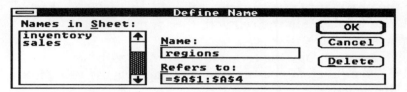

- Type a name in the Name box. If there is text in the cell or cells you have selected, *Excel* proposes a name.
- Next, type the cell reference, formula, or value in the Refers To box in the left-hand side of the formula bar. You may select a cell instead of typing in its name. (If the dialog box is covering a cell you wish to select, you can move it by pressing Alt–Space bar–M.) *Excel* will once again propose an entry for you.
- Choose OK.

  To edit a name:
- Choose the Define Name command and *Excel* displays the names you have already defined.
- Select the name you wish to edit. *Excel* displays the name in the Name box and its reference in the Refers To box.
- You can then edit either the name or its reference.

  To delete a name:
- Select the name you wish to eliminate from the list box.
- Choose the delete button. This does not affect any formulas or values containing the name. It simply removes the name and replaces it with #NAME? .

Create Names Command (Full Menus)
- Alt-R-C
Or
- Ctrl + Shift + F3

You can name many sections of a worksheet simultaneously with the Create Names command.

To use this command:
- Select a range of cells you wish to name. (*Excel* looks along the edges of the cell range for a list of names, and applies them to the cells you wish to name.)
- Choose Create Names from the Formula menu.
- A dialog appears with the options Top Row, Left Column, Bottom Row, or Right Column:

    In *Top Row,* the text in each cell of the top row of the selected range is used to name the column below it.

    In *Bottom Row,* the text in each cell of the bottom row of the selected range is used to name the column above it.

    In *Left Column,* the text in each cell of the left column of the selected range is used to name the row to the right of it.

    In *Right Column,* the text in each cell of the right column of the selected range is used to name the row to the left of it.
- Choose OK.

Figure 1-18. The Create Names Dialog Box

You may also select any combination of these options. If your selections overlap, and there is text in the corner cell, that text will be incorporated into the name for that range.

Apply Names Command (Full Menus)
♦ Alt-R-A

Excel looks for references in the selected cells, and replaces those references with names that are already defined. If you want *Excel* to search for references to replace over the entire worksheet, select only a single cell.

To use this command:
- Select the cell range where you want the references replaced with names.
- Choose Apply Names from the Formula menu.
- Choose the name(s) you want applied from the list box that appears.
- Select the options you want.
- Choose OK.

Figure 1-19. The Apply Names Dialog Box

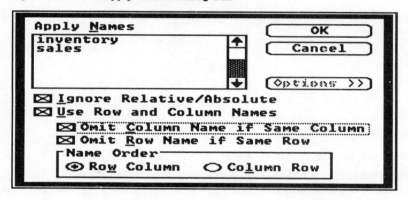

Ignore Relative/Absolute is an option which allows *Excel* to replace the references with names regardless of whether the references are relative or absolute. Most references happen to be relative, and most name definitions happen to be absolute, so turning this option off results in only a few references being replaced by names. It is only a concern if you plan to move or copy the pertinent cells.

Use Row and Column Names is an option which causes *Excel* to use defined names for rows or columns containing the referred-to cell if that individual cell does not have a name.

If this option is chosen, you get more options for using a column or row name if the cell with the formula is contained in the same column or row as the referred-to cell. Another option allows you to specify in what order to list two labels if the referred-to cell has both a row name and a column name.

Note Command
♦ Alt-R-N
Or
♦ Shift + F2

You may attach information regarding specific cells with this command. First select the cell; then use the Note command. In one box, a list of all notes and their associated cells is found. In another box, the complete text of the active cell can be entered or edited.

Figure 1-20. The Note Dialog Box

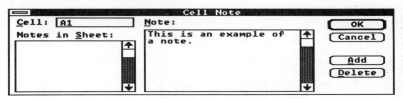

The Add selection adds the text in the box to the cell without exiting the dialog box. The Delete selection deletes text formerly attached to a cell. It does not affect the actual cell. Selecting OK adds the text and exits the dialog box, while Cancel exits the dialog box without accepting changes you have made.

You can attach notes to more than one cell at a time by entering new cells into the Cell box, typing in the note, then using the Add selection to stay in the dialog box rather than exiting with OK.

Goto Command
♦ Alt-R-G
Or
♦ F5

Rather than scroll a worksheet to find a cell, you can use the Goto command.

To use this command:
• Choose Goto from the Formula menu.
• When you choose this command, a list box appears. You can

35

select a name from the box or type in a cell reference.
- Choose OK, and the designated cell appears on your worksheet as the active cell.

You can also select a range rather than a specific area, in which case the upper left cell of that area becomes active.

The Reference option provides a handy way to go back and forth between two areas of a large worksheet. *Excel* remembers where you came from when you last used the Goto command, and places that in the Reference box. Therefore, you can continually use Goto to alternate back and forth between two areas.

Find Command
- ◆ Alt-R-F
Or
- ◆ Shift + F5
- ◆ Shift + F7 (Find previous cell)
- ◆ F7 (Find next cell)

You can locate text and values within a cell, formula, or note by using the Find command. Select a range of cells to search, or search the entire worksheet by selecting only a single cell.

To use this command:
- Select the cell(s) you want to search.
- Choose the Find command. A dialog box appears.
- In the Find What box, type in what it is you want to locate. You may type in any combination of operators (= < >), but they will be treated as text. You may also use the standard DOS wild cards (? *). If you wish to search for a question mark or an asterisk, precede each by a tilde (~? and ~*).

Figure 1-21. The Find Dialog Box

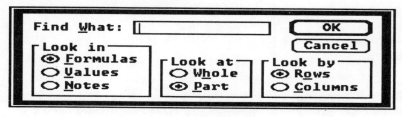

The Look In box gives you the option of searching formulas, values, or notes. The Look At box allows you to indicate whether you want to search for the entire formula or value that corresponds to the text entered in the Find What box, or just part of it. For example, if you specify 35 as the value to search and then select the Whole option, *Excel* will only locate entries consisting wholly of the number 35. However, if you select the Part option, it will also locate entries that contain 35, such as 356, in addition to entries consisting of the number 35 alone.

The Look By option allows you to specify in what order to search. If you choose Rows, *Excel* goes horizontally through the rows. If you choose Columns, *Excel* searches vertically. This is relevant when you want to find more than one occurrence of something. To find the next occurrence, press Enter or click the OK box. To find the previous occurrence, hold down the shift key while pressing Enter or clicking the OK button.

• To start the search, choose OK.

Replace Command (Full Menus)
♦ Alt-R-E

Excel will find all cells that match whatever you type in, and replace that material with whatever you specify. The Find options are the same as described above.

Figure 1-22. The Replace Dialog Box

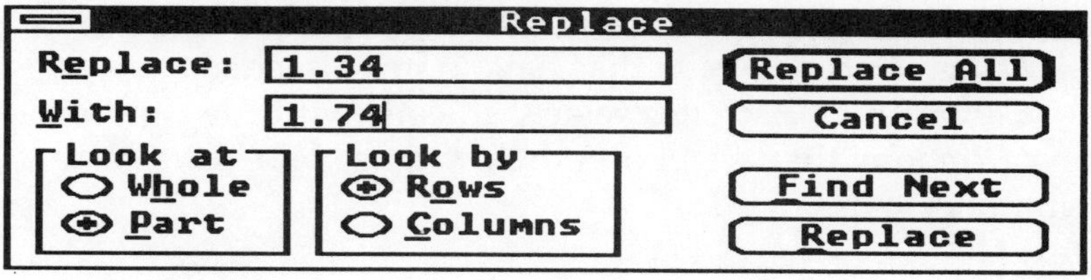

The Replace All option replaces all occurrences with whatever you specify. The Cancel option exits the dialog box and the command. The Find Next option finds the next occurrence of the characters in the Replace box. The previous occurrence can also be found by choosing Find Next while holding down the shift key. The Replace option executes the replacement, assuming the active cell matches whatever the program was searching for.

Select Special Command (Full Menus)
♦ Alt-R-S
Or
♦ Ctrl + ? * / ! | [ ]

This command selects cells or ranges of cells, even discontinuous ranges, with certain characteristics that you specify. It will search within a range that is activated when the command is chosen. Or, if only a single cell is activated, it will search the entire worksheet.

Figure 1-23. The Select Special Dialog Box

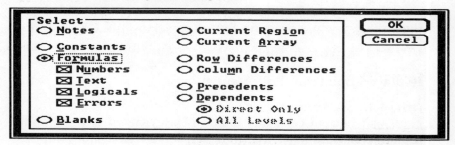

To use this command:
• Choose Select Special from the Formula menu.
• A dialog box appears with the following options.

Notes selects all cells that have notes attached.

Constants or *Formulas* selects all cells with the combination of options that are chosen below those labels:
• Numbers
• Text
• Logicals
• Errors

Blanks selects all blank cells.

Current Region selects a group of cells bordering the active cell that are in turn bordered by blank cells or the worksheet border.

Current Array selects the array to which the active cell belongs, if any.

Row Differences and *Column Differences* compare rows or columns of cells with the activated cell for differences. Any different cell in the same row or column, depending on which is chosen, will be selected.

Precedents selects all cells that the activated cells refer to in their formulas.

Dependents selects all cells that refer to the activated cell in their formulas. Both commands can be acted upon by the Direct Only and All Levels options:

• *Direct Only* selects only cells that are directly referred to in formulas.
• *All Levels* looks at the referred-to cells for other references and selects the cells in those references as well, and carries on until all cells, whether directly or indirectly referred to in formulas related to the activated cells, are selected.
• When you have selected the appropriate options, choose OK.

Format Menu

Figure 1-24. The Format Menu

```
┌────────────┐
│ Format     │
├────────────┴──────────┐
│   Number...           │
│   Alignment...        │
│   Font...             │
│   Border...           │
│   Cell Protection...  │
├───────────────────────┤
│   Row Height...       │
│   Column Width...     │
├───────────────────────┤
│   Justify             │
└───────────────────────┘
```

You can add a polished, professional touch to worksheets with the use of the commands in the Format menu.

Number Command
♦ Alt-T-N
Or
♦ Ctrl + ˜ ! @ # $ % ^

Figure 1-25. The Number Command Dialog Box

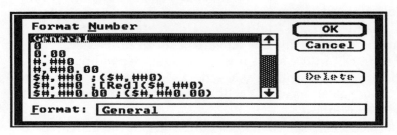

The Number command determines how a number, date, or time is displayed in a cell.

To use this command:
• Select the cell(s) you want to format.
• Choose Number from the Format menu.
• A dialog box appears with formatting choices. You can choose one of these or create your own.
• Choose OK.

To create your own format, select the cells you want to format, click the Number command, type over the list that appears with the symbols that indicate how you want the values to look, and then press Enter or click the OK button.

If you do not use the Number command, *Excel* automatically uses the General format, which basically displays numbers precisely as you entered them.

A wide variety of date and time formats are also listed in the List box.

Alignment Command
♦ Alt-T-A
Or
♦ Ctrl + 1 2 3 4

The Alignment command lets you select from five cell-alignment options: General, Left, Center, Right, and Fill.

If you do not use this command, *Excel* uses the General alignment, which aligns text to the left and numbers to the right.

The Left, Center, and Right options align the contents of the selected cells to the direction indicated.

The Fill option is a fast method of repeating characters throughout a cell. For example, if you type in a (-) and use the Fill option, the dashes are repeated across the cell (or range of cells) selected.

Figure 1-26. The Alignment Dialog Box

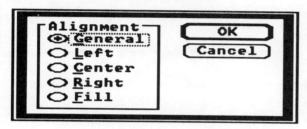

To use the Alignment command:
• Select the cells you want to align.
• Select the Alignment command.
• Choose an option.
• Choose OK.

Font Command
♦ Alt-T-F
Or
♦ Ctrl + 1 2 3 4

Select the font styles contained on the worksheet with this command. As many as four different fonts are available at any one time, and these four slots can be filled with a long list of fonts, accessed by using the Fonts option.

To use this command:
• Select the cell or range of cells for which you wish to pick a font.
• Choose the Font command from the Format menu.
• Select from the four fonts displayed, or use the Fonts option for more selections. The exact number of selections depends on whether you are choosing for the screen display or, if the

Printer Fonts option is selected, for printout. Various printers can handle various fonts. *Excel* knows which fonts your printer can print.
• Choose OK.

Figure 1-27. The Fonts Dialog Box

If you have already defined certain cells with a particular font, and then you rotate that font out of the four slots available, all defined cells will change to the new font put into the slot. Slot number 1 is the default setting for the worksheet, so if you replace that font, then all nondefined cells will display the new font in the first slot. Use the Replace option to replace a slotted font with another font without affecting the selected cells.

Border Command
♦ Alt-T-B

The Border command adds solid border lines and/or shading to the selected cells. This allows you to add emphasis to the standard gridlines.

After you've chosen the Border command, a dialog box appears with a number of options:
• *Outline* puts a border around the outermost edges of the selected area.
• *Left, Right, Top,* and *Bottom* put borders on the corresponding edge of each cell in the range.
• *Shading* puts a series of dots throughout the selected area.

You can use any combination of these options.

Figure 1-28. The Border Dialog Box

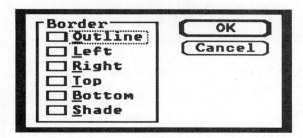

To add a border or shading:
• Select the desired range of cells.
• Select the Border command.
• Choose among the options.
• Choose OK.

Cell Protection Command (Full Menus)
`◆ Alt-T-P`

You can control whether a formula in a selected area is displayed in the formula bar, and whether or not it can be edited, with the Cell Protection command. This command is used in conjunction with the Protect Document command on the Options menu. The options on this menu, Locked and Hidden, do not take effect until the document is password-protected with the Protect Document command.

To use this command:
• Choose the Cell Protection command from the Format menu.
• A dialog box appears giving you the options of Locked and/or Hidden cell protection.

Figure 1-29. The Cell Protection Dialog Box

Locked cells cannot be edited once you've protected a worksheet using the Protect Document command on the Options menu. Initially all cells are locked. This feature is often used to prevent accidental changes. To unlock the cells in the selection choose the Locked option, removing the X.

The Hidden option hides formulas in the selected area of a protected worksheet, preventing them from appearing in the formula bar.

• Select one or both of these options and then choose OK.

Row Height Command
♦ Alt-T-R

The height of a row can be changed using this command.

Figure 1-30. The Row Height Dialog Box

To use this command:
• Select a cell from the row that you wish to set.
• Choose the Row Height command. A dialog box appears with Column Width and Standard Width options. In the Row Height box, *Excel* proposes a number. You can select this or type in your own. The units of measurement are points, the same units that are used to size fonts.

You can hide a row by setting its height to 0. The Standard Height option sets the height to accommodate the tallest font in the row. If you set the height to a size smaller than a font, the letters will appear clipped.
• Choose OK.

The height can be changed with a mouse by dragging the line below the row heading.

Column Width Command
♦ Alt-T-C

You can select the width of designated columns with the Column Width command. You need only select one cell and the Column Width command applies to all the cells in that column. If you select an entire row of cells, the Column Width command applies to all the columns in the worksheet.

Figure 1-31. The Column Width Dialog Box

```
┌─────────────────────────────────────────────────────┐
│                                                       │
│  Column Width: │8.43│        ( ─── OK ─── )          │
│  ⊠ Standard Width            ( Cancel )               │
│                                                       │
└─────────────────────────────────────────────────────┘
```

To use this command:
• Select the columns whose width you want to change.
• Choose the Column Width command.

  A dialog box appears with Column Width and Standard Width options. In the Column Width box, *Excel* proposes a number. You can select this or type in your own. Or you can click the Standard Width box, which fills in about 8.5, depending on which font you've selected as the default. Using the default font as a measure, this means you can squeeze in 8 characters.
• Choose OK.

  To change the column width using the mouse, drag the line to the right of the column you wish to adjust.

Justify Command (Full Menus)
♦ Alt-T-J

The purpose of this command is to take a block of text and spread it more or less evenly over the range you select.

  To use this command:
• Type text in a cell. Don't worry about its extending beyond the border of the cell. If you run out of room, continue in the

cell below it. If you wish to leave a space between paragraphs, skip a cell and then continue. When you've finished, the text should be contained in a column of cells.

- Now select the range over which you'd like the text to appear. All cells that don't contain text should be blank. The column of text should provide the left-hand border of the range, although it's not necessary to use the entire height. Instead, you may wish to spread it more horizontally than vertically. You pick the shape with the cell range selection you make.
- Next, choose the Justify command. If the shape you have picked cannot contain the text, *Excel* will ask you if it's all right to extend the range by adding more rows to the bottom. If you inadvertently overwrite data with text, you can use the Undo command on the Edit menu to undo the justification.

The end result will be the block of text justified within the range. The right margin will be ragged, and paragraphs will probably end with a shortened line.

Data Menu

Figure 1-32. The Data Menu

```
┌─────────┐
│  Data   │
├─────────┴──────────────┐
│   Form...              │
├────────────────────────┤
│  Find                  │
│  Extract...            │
│  Delete                │
│  Set Database          │
│  Set Criteria          │
├────────────────────────┤
│  Sort...               │
├────────────────────────┤
│  Series...             │
│  Table...              │
│  Parse...              │
└────────────────────────┘
```

You can set up a database and then create tables and series, and sort information within it, using the commands in the Data menu.

Form Command
♦ Alt-D-O

This command takes individual records in a database and displays them in a form which facilitates viewing, editing, adding, deleting, and finding records that match the criteria you enter.

A database must first be defined (see below); then this command can be used to bring up the dialog box containing the form. You may select options in the box for accomplishing any of the functions listed above.

The form supplied may be redesigned by creating a macro with a dialog box description. The name Data_Form is then defined on the worksheet to refer to that macro.

Once your data form is created, you can use the keyboard in the following manner:

Action	Key(s) Pressed
To move to the next field in the record	Tab
To move to the previous field in the record	Shift + Tab
To move to the first field in the next record	Enter
To move to the same field in the next record	Down key
To move to the first field of the previous record	Shift + Enter
To move to the same field in the previous record	Up key
To move to the same field ten records forward	Page Down
To move to the same field ten records back	Page Up
To move to the new record at the end of the database	Ctrl + Page Down
To move to the first record	Ctrl + Page Up

You can also use the mouse to move around in the records:

Action	Mouse Action
To select a field	Click in the text box
To move to the same field in the next record	Click the down arrow
To move to the same field in the previous record	Click the up arrow
To move to the same field ten records forward	Click the scroll bar below the scroll box
To move to the same field ten records back	Click the scroll bar above the scroll box
To move to the new record at the end of the database	Drag the scroll box to the bottom
To move to the first record	Drag the scroll box to the top

Find Command
♦ Alt-D-F

The Find command enables you to locate and retrieve records in your database. However, you must first define your database range and criteria range. (These two commands are explained below.)

Once you have chosen the Find command, *Excel* begins searching for the records in the database that match the criteria you selected in the criteria range. If *Excel* cannot locate any records, it displays an alert.

Scrolling is somewhat different when used with the Find command. The scroll boxes in both scroll bars are striped instead of white, and the scroll box shows your relative position in the database range rather than in the entire worksheet. You cannot use the horizontal scroll bar to scroll beyond the right or the left boundary of the database.

You can use other commands when Find is in effect; however, as soon as you do so, you exit Find. The last matching record you found stays displayed.

Another way to exit Find is by clicking Exit Find from the Data menu, or clicking a cell outside of the database range.

You can search backwards in the database for records by holding down the shift key when selecting Find.

Extract Command (Full Menus)
♦ Alt-D-E

The Extract command locates database records that match the defined criteria, and copies the information onto another part of the worksheet.

First, define a criteria range with the Set Criteria command. Then define the area where you want *Excel* to put the extracted records. In this area type or copy the field names you want to extract; then click the Extract command, and a dialog box appears. Within this box you have the option of checking Unique Records Only. Click this box if you want *Excel* to include only one copy of each matching record in the extracted list. Otherwise, if a record meets more than one defined criteria, duplicates of it may be produced.

If the area you selected is not large enough to accommodate the extracted information, an alert appears, indicating that the range is full. Alternately, you can select only the field names as the Extract range, and *Excel* uses all the space it needs down to the bottom of the worksheet.

Using this method, *existing data beneath the field names might be erased without warning and the erasure cannot be undone.* So take care to make sure that there is no data in the cells beneath the field names, or else select a range that includes more than just the field names so that you will receive a warning message.

Delete Command (Full Menus)
♦ Alt-D-D

You can use the Delete command to delete records from the database that meet the criteria defined in the criteria range.

To use this command:
• Define a criteria range containing criteria for records you wish to delete.
• Choose the Delete command.
• Choose OK.

All records that match the criteria are deleted and the rest of the database is shifted up to close the gap.

This command cannot be undone. Therefore, it is a good idea to use the Find command beforehand to see precisely what records *Excel* will delete. Be careful not to include any blank rows in the criteria range, because *Excel* then matches every record in the database.

Set Database Command
♦ Alt-D-B

Use the Set Database command to define the range of cells that will contain a database. The first row of the database contains the field names. You can use any range of cells and as many columns and rows as you wish.

To define a database:
- Select the desired area.
- Choose Set Database.

Excel will then name the range *Database*.

When you choose a Database command *Excel* searches for the name *Database* in order to know which area to act on. Therefore, to alleviate confusion, you may only have one database per worksheet.

Set Criteria Command
♦ Alt-D-C

The criteria *Excel* uses to find, extract, or delete matching records is defined with the Set Criteria command.

Any area on the worksheet outside of the database range can be selected for the criteria range. The top row of this range contains the criteria names, which are either database field names or descriptions of formulas, depending upon whether the type of criteria is comparison or computed, respectively. The rows below it contain the criteria. After you have selected this area, click the Set Criteria command.

If you are using comparison criteria, the criteria names are the same as the names of the fields you want to search. You can simply copy and paste your field names from the database range into the Criteria Name row. These names can be comprised of text or of formulas that produce text.

If you are using computed criteria, use text that describes the formulas you will use as the computed criteria. You cannot use field names with computed criteria.

Next, type the criteria below each criteria name. Type the specific information you wish to locate with comparison criteria. For computed criteria, type a formula. When you're using the Find, Extract, or Delete commands from the Data menu, the criteria will be matched. Note that the Database Form is completely independent of this criteria.

Sort Command
♦ Alt-D-S

To sort the rows or columns within your database range, use the Sort command. Be sure not to include the field name in your selection, as this will cause *Excel* to sort the field names with your records.

   To sort:
• Select the area you wish to sort.
• Choose the Sort command. *Excel* displays a Sort dialog box.

Figure 1-33. The Sort Dialog Box

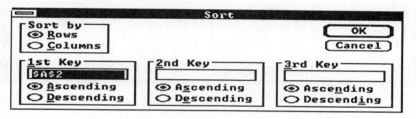

The selections you make in this box indicate to *Excel* which fields in the database to search, and in what order. Click Rows to sort by rows, or Columns to sort by columns. The Key option indicates which column to sort by when sorting rows, or which row to sort by when sorting by columns. You can specify as many as three different keys. If data is identical in the first key, the second key is used to determine the sort order. If data is also identical in the second key, the third key is used.

   If you select the Ascending option, *Excel* sorts the numbers first, followed by the text, then the logical and error values, and finally the blank cells. The Descending option reverses this order, except for blank cells, which will still be sorted last.

• After choosing from among these options, choose OK.

   Data does not have to be defined as a database in order for you to use the Sort command.

Series Command (Full Menus)
♦ Alt-D-R

To fill a group of cells with a series of numbers or dates, use the Series command.

    To use this command:
• Select the rows or columns you want to fill.
• Choose the Series command. *Excel* displays the Series dialog box shown in Figure 1-34.

Figure 1-34. The Series Dialog Box

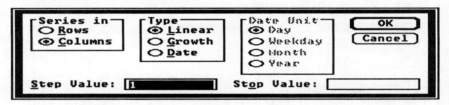

The Series In option indicates which direction you want the fill to follow. If you choose Rows, *Excel* uses the first value in each row to fill the cells in each row of the selection. The Columns option uses the value in the top cell of the column to fill the cells in each column of the selection.

    Next you need to indicate what type of data series you want to create. The type options are used in conjunction with the Step Value and Stop Value entries at the bottom of the dialog box.

    If you select the Linear option, *Excel* adds the Step Value to the values in your worksheet. The Step Value is the amount you entered in the box, indicating how much you want the series to be increased. The Stop Value indicates where you want the series to end. The Growth option multiplies the value of each cell by the Step Value.

    The Date option is used to activate the Date Unit box. The option you select in this box tells *Excel* the unit according to which you want the series of dates to increase.

• After you have selected all the appropriate options, choose OK.

Table Command
♦ Alt-D-T

It's possible to perform what-if analyses by changing certain constant values on your worksheet and noting the effect on formula values. For example, you can determine what your monthly loan payments will be at different interest rates by substituting each interest rate in the formula. However, this can be very time-consuming. It is quicker to design a table and then use the Table command to analyze the changes in values.

This command enables you to build two kinds of tables: one-input tables, which use one variable (as in the above example), and two-input tables, which use two variables. To use our example, suppose you wanted to know what your loan payments would be, not only for varying interest rates, but for varying principal amounts as well. For this you would make a two-input table.

To make a one-input table, make a list of all the input values down a column. In our example, we might choose to list 9, 9.5, 10, 10.5, 11, 11.5, and 12 percent. Leave space to the right of this list, since this is where the values will appear. At the head of the column to the right of the list, enter the formula used to calculate the payments. Where the interest rate would go in the formula, make that a reference to any available cell outside the table area. In that cell, enter an interest rate—it doesn't matter which one you enter.

Now select the table range—the column of interest rates and the column next to it, including the formula at the top. Next, use the Table command. A dialog box will appear. Since the data is listed in a column, enter the input cell (the cell where the interest rate is) in the Column Input Cell box. Press Enter or click the OK button. *Excel* now fills in the table with the results of the formula for the various input values.

Figure 1-35. The Table Dialog Box

Creating a two-input table is very similar, except that the formula goes at the top of the list of interest rates (using our example), and the second-input values (the various principal amounts) go in that same row to the right of the formula. In other words, the formula goes at the upper left-hand corner of the table. Pick a cell outside the table area, and put a principal amount in it. For example, you might put $30,000 in that cell, and list amounts from $10,000 to $40,000 across the top of the table. Modify the formula to refer to the cell you picked for the principal amount.

Now we'll create the table. Select the table range and use the Table command. In addition to the input cell being identified in the Column Input Cell box, the second cell's address goes in the Row Input Cell box. Press Enter or click the OK button, and the values fill in the table.

Parse Command (Full Menus)
♦ Alt-D-P

This command is useful when you import data from other applications into *Excel*. Sometimes material that should be in different cells appears strung together in one cell. With Parse you can select where the cell divisions should occur, and divide the remainder of the cells in the manner you specify.

To use this command:
• First, select the range you wish to parse. It can be any number of rows, but should be only one column wide.
• Next, choose the Parse command. The first cell's contents appear in a special dialog box. You can now insert brackets where you would like the cells to be divided.

Figure 1-36. The Parse Dialog Box

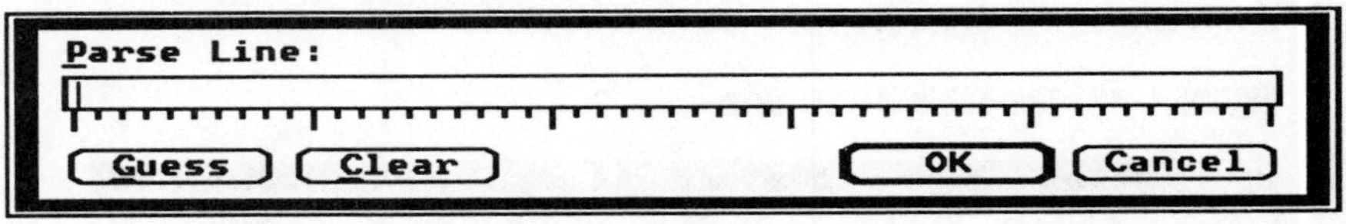

If you want, you can choose Guess, and *Excel* places the brackets where it guesses they should go. You may then adjust them from there.

• Press Enter or click OK, and the dividing will be done on the remainder of the cells in the range.

Press Escape or click Cancel to exit without dividing the cells.

Options Menu

Figure 1-37. The Options Menu

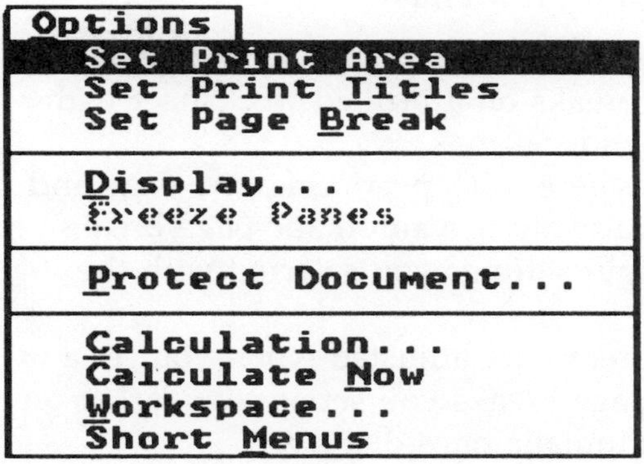

```
| Options |
   Set Print Area
   Set Print Titles
   Set Page Break

   Display...
   Freeze Panes

   Protect Document...

   Calculation...
   Calculate Now
   Workspace...
   Short Menus
```

With the Options menu commands you can make changes that affect characteristics of the entire worksheet.

Set Print Area Command
♦ Alt-O-A

With the Set Print Area command you can print a portion of a worksheet, as opposed to the entire document.

To use this command:
• Select the area you want to print.
• Choose Set Print Area. *Excel* will name this area Print_Area.
• Next, choose Print from the File menu.

If you want to return to printing the entire worksheet, use the Define Name command to delete the name Print_Area.

Set Print Titles Command (Full Menus)
♦ Alt-O-T

The Set Print Titles command enables you to specify rows and columns to be printed as titles when you print your worksheet.

The rows you specify print at the top of every page containing these cells, and the columns you specify print at the left of every page containing these cells.

To specify the titles you want to print, designate the rows and/or columns that contain the titles you want. You then choose the Set Print Titles command, and choose OK.

Set Page Break Command (Full Menus)
♦ Alt-O-B

You can set manual page breaks on a printed worksheet with the Set Page Break command.

Page breaks indicate where to stop printing one page and begin with another. *Excel* already has automatic page breaks that are based on the margin settings you selected with the Page Setup command.

The automatic page breaks are adjusted when you set a manual page break. The page breaks you set appear darker on the worksheet than the automatic ones displayed.

Page breaks are inserted above and to the left of the active cell.

Remove Page Break Command
The page breaks you set remain on a worksheet until they are eliminated with the Remove Page Break command.

To remove manual page breaks:
• Select any cell directly to the right of or below the break.
• Click the Remove Page Break command.

If the active cell is not to the right of or below the break, the command is dimmed.

Display Command
♦ Alt-O-D
Or
♦ Ctrl + ' (formulas/values toggle)

You can control the display of formulas, gridlines, row and column headings, and zero values with the Display command.

When you select this command a dialog box appears with four boxes. If you select the Formulas box, the cells display formulas rather than the values they produce. When you select this option, the width of all columns in the affected area is doubled.

Figure 1-38. The Display Dialog Box

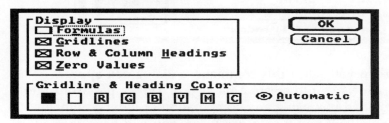

Gridlines are normally displayed on a worksheet; however, you can remove them by unselecting the Gridlines box.

Similarily, to hide normally displayed row and column numbers, unselect the Row and Column Headings box.

Excel normally displays all zero values. However, if you unselect the Zero Values box, all zero values are displayed as blank cells.

At the bottom of the dialog box, you can select gridline and heading colors. These are normally the same as the text color defined in the Control Panel.

The settings in the dialog box only affect the active portion of the worksheet.

Freeze Panes Command (Full Menus)
♦ Alt-O-F

This command freezes one pane of a split window while you can scroll freely in the other pane. Panes to the left of a vertical split do not scroll horizontally. Panes above a horizontal split do not scroll vertically.

To use this command:
• Choose Freeze Panes.

Protect Document/ Unprotect Document Commands (Full Menus)
♦ Alt-O-P

You can protect your worksheet from unintentional changes with the Protect Document command.

Figure 1-39. The Protect Document Dialog Box

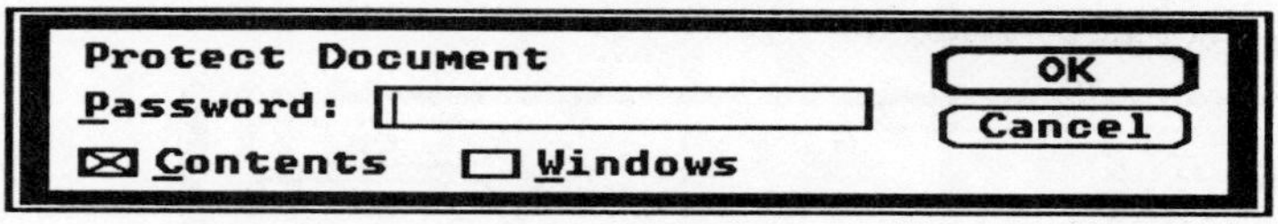

```
┌──────────────────────────────────────────────────┐
│  Protect Document              ┌─────────────┐   │
│  Password: │                │  │     OK      │   │
│                                └─────────────┘   │
│  ☒ Contents    ☐ Windows       ( Cancel )        │
└──────────────────────────────────────────────────┘
```

When you select this command a dialog box appears which allows you to create a password. Type a password into the provided box using any combination of letters, numbers, and symbols. If you type a password, you will have to use the same password to unprotect the document.

Protecting a document is beneficial if you want other people to use your worksheet models without the ability to edit them. However, if you are merely protecting your worksheet from any unintentional changes you may make yourself, you are better off not using a password, as you will have to recall it in order to use the Unprotect Document command.

To protect a worksheet:
• Select the cells you want to protect.
• Tell *Excel* how you want them protected with the Cell Protection command from the Format menu.
• Next, choose the Protect Document command and type in a password if you have chosen to use one.
• Choose OK.

The Protect Document command will then change to Unprotect Document on the Options menu. To unprotect a document, choose this command. If you used a password to protect the document, type it in and then choose OK. If you did not use a password, simply choose OK.

Calculation Command
• Alt-O-C

Depending upon the length of a worksheet, calculations can sometimes take a long time, even though *Excel* recalculates as few cells as possible when a number is changed. The Calculation command is used to turn off automatic calculation so that speedy data entry can be accomplished without your having to wait for recalculation.

Figure 1-40. The Calculation Dialog Box

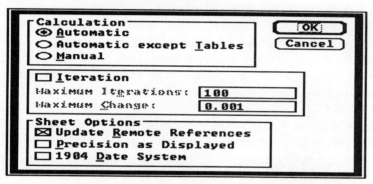

The dialog box contains three sub-boxes. In the first, you can choose among Automatic (the default setting), where *Excel* calculates everything, Automatic Except Tables, which can speed things up because tables take the longest time to calculate, and Manual, which causes calculation only when the Calculate Now command on the Options menu is chosen.

When a formula acts upon itself in a never-ending cyclical fashion, this is known as *iteration*. The second sub-box allows you to specify a limit on iterations. You can choose the limit to be either the number of iterations, or the maximum change per iteration. If you fill in both boxes, *Excel* halts the iterations at the first of the two values reached.

The third sub-box has three miscellaneous options. The first, Update Remote References, deals with references in the worksheet that refer to an outside application. If this box is not checked, the worksheet displays the last value it received from the remote application and does not continually update that value.

The Precision as Displayed option tells *Excel* to ignore its usual 15-digit accuracy and only calculate to as many digits as you've chosen to display. For example, if you are using a dollars and cents format, accuracy in calculations will only be to two decimal places to the right of the decimal point. Ordinarily, accuracy will be to 15 places total, even though fewer places are actually displayed.

This difference will often result in a difference in the result of a calculation. For example, if you divide 100 by 6 and display the answer in dollars and cents, it will be $16.67. Ordinarily, if you then multiplied this by 1000, the result would be $16666.67 (even though 16.67 is displayed, *Excel* stores a far more accurate number in its memory). However, if the Precision as Displayed option is chosen, the result is $16670.00 (16.67 * 1000).

The 1904 Date System option is primarily used for converting Apple Macintosh *Excel* worksheets to the IBM *Excel* format. This normally happens automatically, but if for some reason your dates are off by four years, select this option.

Calculate Now/Calculate Document Command
♦ Alt-O-N
Or
♦ Shift + F9
Or
♦ Ctrl + =

These commands are used in conjunction with the Calculation command described above. When Calculation is set to manual, Calculate Now, when chosen, actually performs the calculating.

If you hold down the shift key when choosing the Options menu, Calculate Document (Alt-O-N or F9) appears in place of Calculate Now. This option calculates only the active document instead of all documents open at the time.

Workspace Command

♦ Alt-O-W

With this command you may choose options that affect how the workspace is displayed and how it interacts with you.

The Fixed Decimal option allows entry of numbers without the need to press the decimal-point key. For example, if you choose 2 (moving the decimal point two spaces to the left), and enter 1290, the number becomes 12.90. You may also enter a negative number here; -2 would result in 129000 (moving the decimal point two spaces to the right).

The R1C1 option changes the normal A1 style of cell addressing to a different format. The *Excel* default is the A1 reference style, which uses numbers for row references and letters for column references. A1 thus indicates column A, row 1. The R1C1 reference style, on the other hand, displays the row reference first, and then the column reference. It also uses numbers for columns, rather than letters. Using this method A1 translates to R1C1, D3 to R3C4, and so on. Some users who have experience with other spreadsheets prefer this kind of formatting.

Figure 1-41. The Workspace Dialog Box

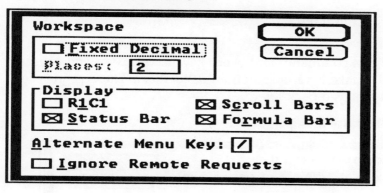

You may choose to not display the Scroll bars, Status bar, and/or Formula bar by unchecking these options.

Normally you access the menu bars with the Alt key. If you prefer a different key, type it in the Alternate Menu Key box.

Ignore Remote Requests deals with *Excel's* relationship to other applications. If such a relationship has been set up, checking this box denies the outside application access to your worksheet.

Short Menus/Full Menus
This command is described at the beginning of the chapter.

Macro Menu

Figure 1-42. The Macro Menu

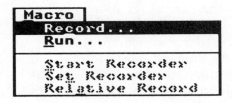

Routine functions can be minimized with the use of macros. A macro is a series of commands and functions that, when calculated, carry out a sequence of actions. You name, define, and run macros with the commands in the Macro menu.

Record Command
♦ Alt-M-C

Select this command, and every keystroke/action you subsequently make is recorded on a macro sheet. These actions can then be played back later.

Figure 1-43. The Record Dialog Box

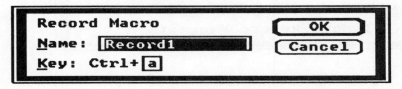

If no macro sheet is open, or if an open macro sheet does not have a range designated, *Excel* opens a new macro sheet to hold the macro.

Run Command
♦ Alt-M-R

The Run command activates defined macros.

After a macro has been created and its macro sheet is open, you may use this command to run the macro. To do so:
• Choose Run from the Macro menu.
• A dialog box appears with a list of defined macros. Select one of the displayed macros and choose OK. The macro then runs.

Macros can also be run by pressing the key defined to make them run, thus avoiding the keystrokes necessary to select this command and to pick a macro from the dialog box.

Start Recorder/Stop Recorder Commands (Full Menus)
♦ Alt-M-S

This command is similar to the Record command, except that the macro range must be already defined in order for you to use this command.

When the recorder is on, every stroke of the keyboard and mouse automatically transfers to the macro sheet as a command.

After you have selected the Start Recorder command, it changes to Stop Recorder on the Macro menu. You can then click the Stop Recorder command to stop recording.

Set Recorder Command (Full Menus)
♦ Alt-M-T

Use the Set Recorder command to designate where you want the macros to go. Simply select an area and then click the Set Recorder command.

If you only select one cell, recording starts in that cell and then continues down the column. Once the bottom of the column is reached, recording is redirected to the top of the next column, and proceeds in the same fashion.

If you select a cell range, recording starts in the upper left corner of the range, and once again proceeds down the column and then is redirected to the top of the next column.

If any cells in the range you select are not blank, they are skipped over, with the exception of a cell containing RE-TURN( ), which is overwritten. This allows you to create lengthy macros in more than one recording session, by appending one set of commands to another set without ending the macro prematurely by inserting the RETURN( ) command.

Absolute Record/Relative Record Commands (Full Menus)
♦ Alt-M-A

Cell references are initially recorded in macros as relative references. You can record them as absolute references by selecting the Absolute Record command.

This will change the command to Relative Record on the Macro menu. You can then select the Relative Record command to go back to using relative references.

Window Menu

Figure 1-44. The Window Menu

The commands in the Window menu enable you to open existing windows and create new ones.

New Window Command
♦ Alt-W-N

You can open a new window on an active worksheet with the New Window command. Extra windows are useful for simultaneously viewing parts of a large worksheet that are widely separated. You can open as many windows as you like, as long as *Excel* has enough memory remaining to accommodate them.

Excel numbers each window for you. However, if you close a window, these numbers can change to keep window numbers consecutive.

Figure 1-45. New Windows

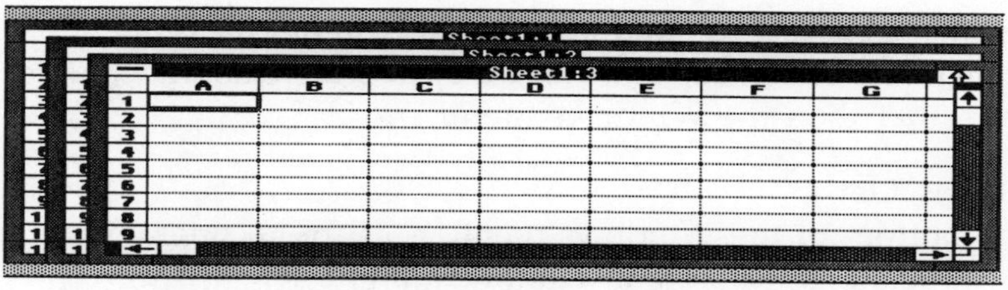

   To use this command:
• Choose New Window from the Window menu.

Show Info/Show Document Command (Full Menus)
♦ Alt-W-S
Or
♦ Shift + F2

Show Info displays a window containing information about the active document if it is a worksheet or a macro sheet. You can redisplay the actual document by selecting Show Document, which appears in place of Show Info when it is activated.

Arrange All Command
This command will rearrange the open windows in *Excel* so that the screen space is used most efficiently.

   To use this command:
• Choose the Arrange All command from the Window menu.

65

Hide/Unhide Commands (Full Menus)
♦ Alt-W-H (Hide)
♦ Alt-W-U (Unhide)

It can be useful to hide a window from view while still making use of its data through references and macros. Sometimes the screen becomes cluttered and hard to work with. The Hide command hides the active window from view.

If the Protect Document command from the Options window is activated, you will be asked to supply a password when hiding the window.

The Unhide command reverses the Hide command, displaying the hidden window. If a password was supplied when Hide was used, it is needed in order to Unhide. If no open windows are displayed, the Unhide option appears on the File menu rather than the Windows menu.

Windows List
At the bottom of the Windows menu, a list of all open windows appears. To activate a window, merely select it from the list by typing in its number or clicking it with the mouse.

Help Menu

Figure 1-46. The Help Menu

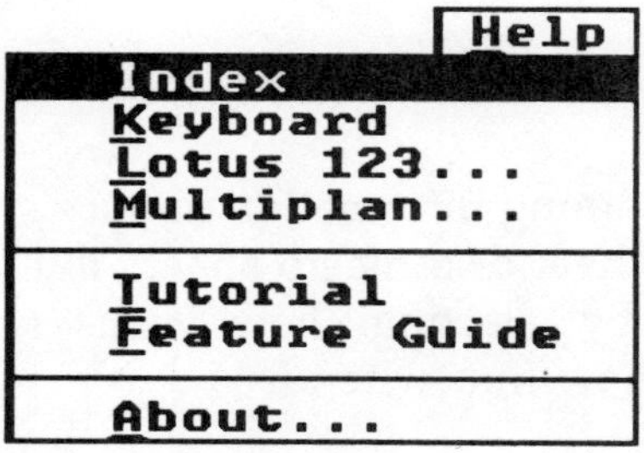

Excel provides an extensive help facility which can be accessed through this menu or by pressing the F1 key at any point in the program. Context-sensitive help can be accessed by holding down the shift key while pressing F1.

Index Command
◆ Alt-H-I
Or
◆ F1
Or
◆ Shift + F1 (Context-sensitive help)

When you've issued this command, a list of topics appears. The topics can be selected with the Tab key or clicked on with the mouse. The index can also be accessed by pressing F1 from within the program.

Keyboard Command
◆ Alt-H-K

Excel Help displays the various keyboard commands, conveniently organized in categories. Many of these commands are shortcuts, and are not evident from perusing the main menus.

Lotus 123 Command
◆ Alt-H-L

Converts *Lotus 1-2-3* commands to *Excel* commands. Simply type in the *Lotus* command, and the program returns the equivalent *Excel* command and any relevant information. You may type in a slash (/) before the *Lotus* command, but it is not required.

Figure 1-47. The Lotus 123 Dialog Box and Command

Lotus 123 Help   [OK]
Command: [/fr]   [Cancel]

Figure 1-48. *Excel* **Returns an Equivalent Command**

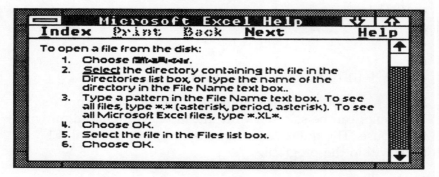

Multiplan Command
♦ Alt-H-M

Converts *Multiplan* commands to *Excel* commands. Simply type in the *Multiplan* command, and the program returns the equivalent *Excel* command and any relevant information.

Tutorial Command
♦ Alt-H-T

This command begins the online *Excel* tutorial, wherein you will find interactive lessons on *Excel*'s basic features. A series of menus branch off to other menus, allowing you to go to any section of the tutorial without having to go through unwanted instruction.

Feature Guide Command
♦ Alt-H-F

Gives a guided tour of *Excel*'s myriad features, along with interactive lessons to familiarize you with the basics of using these features.

About Command
♦ Alt-H-A

Shows how much memory is available, and displays general information about Microsoft *Excel*.

Info Window and Menu

Figure 1-49. The Info Window

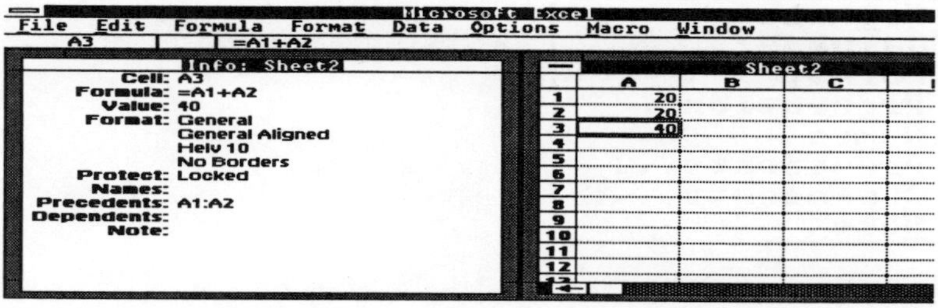

Use the Info Window to view detailed information about the cell that is currently active.

To use the Info Window:

• Choose the Show Info command from the Window menu.

Note that the menu bar changes to display the Info Window menus when you open the Info window. You choose commands here just as you choose them from the Worksheet Menu Bar.

To stop using the Info Window:

• Make the Info Window active and choose Close from the Control menu.

When you use the Info Window you are able to show the following kinds of information about the active cell:

Cell—The active cell reference.

Formula—The formula of the active cell.

Value—The value of the active cell (for example, the result of the formula).

Format—The active cell's formats, such as number, font, alignment, shading, and borders.

Protection—Tells whether the active cell's formula is hidden or whether the cell is locked or unlocked.

Names—The named cell ranges that include the active cell.

Precedents—Any cell that the active cell refers to.

Dependents—Any cell that refers to the active cell.

Note—Any text attacted to the active cell through the Note command.

Figure 1-50. The Info Menu

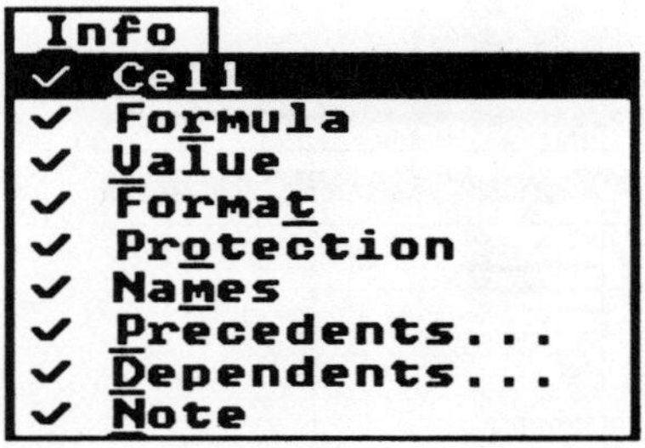

```
┌─Info─┐
│ ✓ Cell        │
│ ✓ Formula     │
│ ✓ Value       │
│ ✓ Format      │
│ ✓ Protection  │
│ ✓ Names       │
│ ✓ Precedents...│
│ ✓ Dependents...│
│ ✓ Note        │
└───────────────┘
```

To select what information is shown in the Info Window:
• Choose the Info menu.
• Choose the command for which you want information.
    Excel marks that command with a check mark and the information appears in the Info Window.

To remove specific information from the Info Window:
• Choose the Info menu.
• Choose the command whose information you want to remove.
    Excel removes the check mark from that command and its information disappears from the Info Window.

To switch between the worksheet and Info Window:
• Choose the window name you want to be active from the bottom of the Window menu.

Chart Menus

The *Excel* Menu Bar changes to reflect the Chart Menu Bar when you choose the Chart option from the New command on the File menu.

To create a chart:
• Select the data you want included in the chart.
• Choose New from the File menu.
• Choose the Chart option from the New command.
• If you want your chart created in a format other than the default, choose the format you want from the Gallery menu.

(When the Gallery dialog box appears, you can preview the various kinds of main charts available, such as Area or Column, by choosing Next or Previous.)

To save a chart:
• Make the chart window active.
• Choose the Save As command from the File menu.
• Type the chart's name in the text box that appears.
• Choose OK.

To print a chart:
• Make the chart window active.
• Choose the Print command from the File menu.
• Choose OK.

Gallery Menu

Gallery Area Command
♦ Alt-G-A

Choose this command when you want to change your current chart format to that of an area chart.

Area charts are useful for comparing relative values of entered data. The different degrees of shading enable you to illustrate subtle trends in a simple, easily understood format. There are five different area chart formats to select from:
• Simple area chart
• 100-percent area chart
• Area chart with vertical lines
• Area chart with gridlines
• Area chart with labels

Figure 1-51. The Gallery Menu

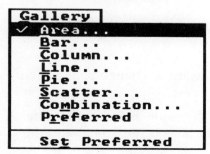

To create an area chart:
- Choose Area from the Gallery menu.
- Choose the kind of area chart you want from the dialog box which appears. (Use the cursor keys to select the different chart boxes.)
- Choose OK.

Gallery Bar Command
♦ Alt-G-B

Choose this command when you want to change your current chart format to that of a bar chart.

Bar charts are best utilized when you want to observe data trends over a certain time period and compare two or more sets of values. You can select a suitable bar chart from seven options:

- Simple bar chart
- Bar chart with varied patterns
- Stacked bar chart
- Overlapped bar chart
- 100-percent stacked bar chart
- Simple bar chart with vertical gridlines
- Simple bar chart with value labels

Any of these can be enhanced with legends, titles, or many other specifications, depending on your needs.

To create a bar chart:
- Choose Bar from the Gallery menu.
- Choose the kind of bar chart you want from the dialog box which appears. (Use the cursor keys to select the different chart boxes.)
- Choose OK.

Gallery Column Command
♦ Alt-G-C

Choose this command when you want to change your current chart format to that of a column chart.

Column charts are basically the same as bar charts. The only difference is that the category axis is horizontal and the

value axis is vertical. You can choose from seven column chart formats:
- Column chart with varied patterns
- Stacked column chart
- Overlapped column chart
- 100-percent stacked column chart
- Simple column chart with horizontal gridlines
- Simple column chart with value labels
- Step chart that displays the columns without spacing

    To create a column chart:
- Choose Column from the Gallery menu.
- Choose the kind of column chart you want from the dialog box which appears. (Use the cursor keys to select the different chart boxes.)
- Choose OK.

Gallery Line Command
- ♦ Alt-G-L

Choose this command when you want to change your current chart format to that of a line chart.

    Line graphs are beneficial for analyzing trends, particularly when you want to illustrate subtle variations. There are seven formats to select from:
- Simple line chart with lines and markers
- Lines only
- Markers only
- Lines and markers with horizontal and vertical gridlines
- Lines and markers with logarithmic scale and gridlines
  - Hi-lo chart with markers
  - Hi-lo chart with lines

    To create a line chart:
- Choose Line from the Gallery menu.
- Choose the kind of line chart you want from the dialog box which appears. (Use the cursor keys to select the different chart boxes.)
- Choose OK.

Gallery Pie Command
♦ Alt-G-P

Choose this command when you want to change your current chart format to that of a pie chart.

The pie chart is excellent for showing the relationship between components of a whole. There are six options for the pie chart:
• Simple pie chart
• Pie chart with all the wedges patterned the same and labeled with categories
• Pie chart with one wedge disconnected from the whole
• Pie chart with all wedges disconnected
• Pie chart with category labels
• Pie chart with percentage labels

To create a pie chart:
• Choose Pie from the Gallery menu.
• Choose the kind of pie chart you want from the dialog box which appears. (Use the cursor keys to select the different chart boxes.)
• Choose OK.

Gallery Scatter Command
♦ Alt-G-S

Choose this command when you want to change your current chart format to that of a scatter chart.

Scattered diagrams are instrumental in depicting the relationship between two characteristics, such as level of education and income. There are five scatter chart formats to select from:
• Scatter chart with markers only
• Scatter chart with markers from the same series connected by lines
• Markers with horizontal and vertical gridlines
• Markers with semi-logarithmic gridlines
• Markers with log-log gridlines

To create a scatter chart:
• Choose Scatter from the Gallery menu.

• Choose the kind of scatter chart you want from the dialog box which appears. (Use the cursor keys to select the different chart boxes.)
• Choose OK.

Gallery Combination Command
♦ Alt-G-M

It is also possible to create your own combination chart. This feature enables you to take an existing chart and add an overlay chart to it. There are four combinations to choose from:
• Column chart with overlaid line chart
• Column chart overlaid by line chart with opposing scale
• Two line charts overlaid with independent scales
• Area chart with overlaid column chart

   To create a combination chart:
• Choose Combination from the Gallery menu.
• Choose the kind of combination chart you want from the dialog box which appears. (Use the cursor keys to select the different chart boxes.)
• Choose OK.

Gallery Preferred Command
♦ Alt-G-R

Use this command to change the current chart's format to the one you have defined with the Gallery Set Preferred command.

Gallery Set Preferred Command
♦ Alt-G-T

Use this command to change *Excel's* default chart format to one of your preference. Once the change is made, choosing the Gallery Preferred Command will change your chart format to the new default.

   To change your preferred format:
• First, change your current chart to reflect the chart format you want as the default.
• Choose the Set Preferred command from the Gallery menu.

Preserve this new chart default by saving your workspace with the Save Workspace command from the File menu (Full menus only).

Chart Menu

Attach Text Command
♦ Alt-C-T

Use this command to attach text to specific parts of your chart. Once the text is attached, you are able to edit it in the formula bar.

To use this command:
• Choose the Attach Text command from the Chart menu.
• Choose the part of the chart you want to add text to from the dialog box that appears.
• Choose OK.

Figure 1-52. The Chart Menu

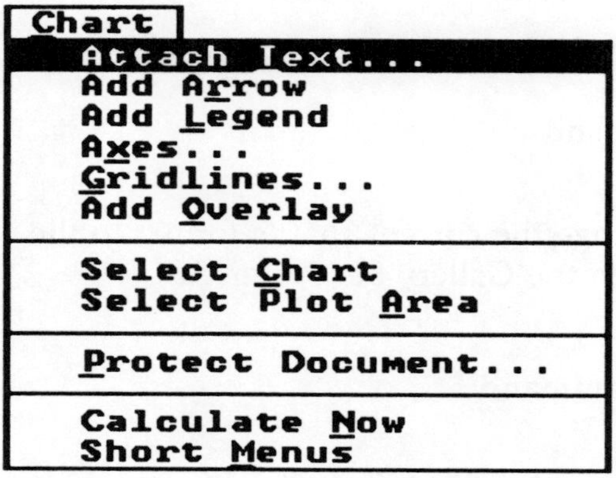

```
┌─────────────────────────────────┐
│ Chart                           │
├─────────────────────────────────┤
│   Attach Text...                │
│   Add Arrow                     │
│   Add Legend                    │
│   Axes...                       │
│   Gridlines...                  │
│   Add Overlay                   │
├─────────────────────────────────┤
│   Select Chart                  │
│   Select Plot Area              │
├─────────────────────────────────┤
│   Protect Document...           │
├─────────────────────────────────┤
│   Calculate Now                 │
│   Short Menus                   │
└─────────────────────────────────┘
```

Excel adds the text, selects it, and displays it in the formula bar, where you are able to edit it as you choose.
• When the text is correct, press Enter to put the text in the chart.

Add Arrow Command
♦ Alt-C-R

This command places an arrow in the upper left-hand corner
of the chart. You are then able to move, size, or format the arrow using the Format Move, Format Size, or Format Patterns
command.

To use this command:
• Make sure the chart window is active.
• Choose the Add Arrow command from the Chart menu.

Add Legend Command
♦ Alt-C-L

Use this command to add a legend to your current chart. After
the legend is added you can format it with the Format Patterns
and Format Font commands.

To use this command:
• Make sure the chart window is active.
• Choose the Add Legend command from the Chart menu.

Axes Command
♦ Alt-C-X

This command determines whether the axes of a chart are
visible.

To use this command:
• Choose Axes from the Chart menu.
• Select the option you want from the dialog box that appears.
• Choose OK.

Gridlines Command
♦ Alt-C-G

This command determines whether the chart's major and mi-
nor gridlines are visible.

To use the Gridlines command:
• Choose the Gridlines command from the Chart menu.
• Select the option you want from the dialog box that appears.
• Choose OK.

Add Overlay Command (Full Menus)
♦ Alt-C-O

This command creates an overlay chart and adds it to your current chart. While the overlay is initially a line chart by default, you can change this format by using the Format Overlay command.

To use the Add Overlay command:
• Choose the Add Overlay command from the Chart menu.

Select Chart Command
♦ Alt-C-C

This command selects the entire chart in the active window. Once the chart is selected, you can use these commands:
Edit Clear
Edit Copy
Format Font
Format Main Chart
Format Overlay (if applicable)
Format Patterns

To use this command:
• Choose the Select Chart command from the Chart menu.

Select Plot Area Command
♦ Alt-C-A

This command selects the plot area of the chart in the active window.

To use it:
• Choose the Select Plot Area command from the Chart menu.

Protect Document Command (Full Menus)
♦ Alt-C-P

Use this command to keep your chart's data series and formats from being altered, and the chart's window from being moved or sized.

To use this command:
- Choose the Protect Document command from the Chart menu.
- Select the options you want from the dialog box that appears:

Password   If you want to password-protect your chart, you can enter as many as 16 characters (any combination of letters, symbols, or numbers) in the password text box. Be warned, however, that if you lose your password you cannot unprotect your chart.

               You can choose OK without entering a password. In this case, you won't need to enter a password to unprotect your chart. Instead, you will need only to choose Unprotect Document from the Chart menu.

Contents   Protect the contents from alteration.

Windows   Protect the windows from alteration.
- Choose OK.

Calculate Now Command
◆ Alt-C-N

Or

◆ F9

The Calculate Now command calculates all open worksheets and redraws any charts dependent on them according to the new values generated.

To use this command:
- Choose Calculate Now from the Chart menu.

Full Menus/Short Menus Command
◆ Alt-C-M

Using this command changes all menus to show all available commands instead of just the ones on the short menus. Once this command is chosen, it changes to Short Menus.

To use this command:
- Choose Full Menus from the Chart menu.

Format Menu

Patterns
♦ Alt-T-P

Use this command to change the appearance of an object in your chart.

Figure 1-53. The Format Menu

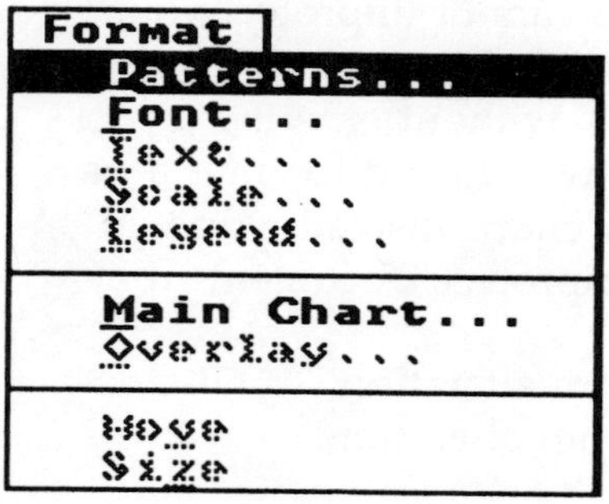

```
┌─────────────────────────────┐
│ Format                      │
├─────────────────────────────┤
│   Patterns...               │
│   Font...                   │
│   Text...                   │
│   Scale...                  │
│   Legend...                 │
├─────────────────────────────┤
│   Main Chart...             │
│   Overlay...                │
├─────────────────────────────┤
│   Move                      │
│   Size                      │
└─────────────────────────────┘
```

To use the Patterns command:
• Select the object(s) you want changed. (To select the whole chart, use the Select Chart command from the Chart menu.)
• Choose Patterns from the Format menu.
• Select the options you want from the dialog box that appears.
• Choose OK.

Font
♦ Alt-T-F

Choosing this command when your chart is the current document ment allows you to change the font of the selected text. Select the entire chart (using the Select Chart command from the Chart menu) before choosing this command to change the font for all text in the chart.

To use this command:
• Choose the Font command from the Format menu.
• Select the font options you want from the dialog box that appears:

Font	Lists the fonts available for your chart.
Size	Lists the sizes available for the fonts.

Style	You can choose any combination of the available font styles.
Printer Fonts	Determines the fonts that are displayed in the Font box.
Background	Determines the appearance of the area behind your text.
Automatic	*Excel* chooses the background pattern for you.
Transparent	Allows you to see what is behind your text.
White Out	Makes white an area (rectangular in shape) large enough to hold your text.

• Choose OK.

Text

♦ Alt-T-T

This command determines the alignment of the selected chart text.

To use this command:
• Select the text.
• Choose the Text command from the Format menu.
• Select the options you want from the dialog box that appears:

Text Alignment	Determines vertical and horizontal alignment of the text within the text border.
Vertical Text	This option stacks text vertically.
Automatic Text	This option restores the original text if it was created using the Attach Text command.
Automatic Size	This option restores the border to automatic size if you have changed it.

• Choose OK.

Scale

♦ Alt-T-S

This command determines the look of the axes, the priority in which the categories or values are arranged, and where the axes cross. The Scale command also determines the interval between tick marks and tick mark labels when the category axis is selected; it determines range of values displayed, the scale used, and whether the scale is logarithmic when the value axis is selected.

To use Scale:
- Select the axis you want to change.
- Choose the Scale command from the Format menu.
- Select the options you want from the dialog box that appears.
- Choose OK.

Legend
♦ Alt-T-L

The Legend command controls the position and orientation of the legend on your chart.

To use this command:
- Choose the Legend command from the Format menu.
- Select the option you want from the dialog box that appears.
- Choose OK.

Main Chart
♦ Alt-T-M

This command determines the main chart's type and its formats. The Type commands that appear in the dialog box are comparable to the commands in the Gallery menu.

To use this command:
- Choose the Main Chart command from the Format menu.
- Select the Type and Format you want from the dialog box that appears.
- Choose OK.

Overlay (Full Menus)
♦ Alt-T-O

Use this command to choose the type and format of your overlay chart.

To use this command:
- Choose the Overlay command from the Format menu.
- Select the type and format of your overlay chart from the dialog box that appears.
- Choose OK.

Move
♦ Alt-T-V

Use this command to move an object in your chart with the keyboard:
• Select the object you want to move.
• Choose the Move command from the Format menu.
• Use the directional cursor keys to move the object.
• Press Enter when you've finished.

Size
♦ Alt-T-Z

Use this command to resize a chart object with the keyboard:
• Select the object you want to resize.
• Choose the Size command from the Format menu.
• Use the directional cursor keys to size the object.
• Press Enter when you've finished.

Chapter 2
How to Use *Excel*

Chapter 2
How to Use *Excel*

Excel offers you a world of features, but before you can take advantage of them, you must learn a few basics.

Using the Keyboard in *Excel*

Moving around the screen

Action	Key
To cancel an action	Escape
To confirm an action	Enter
To move to the beginning of a row	Home
To move to the end of a row	End
To move left, right, up, or down in order to select cells	Directional cursor key
To move your location up by one window	Pg Up
To move your location down by one window	Pg Down
To move your location to the upper left corner of the worksheet	Control + Home
To move your location to the lower right corner of the worksheet	Control + End
To move to the edge of the data block	Control + directional cursor key
To select an entire row	Shift + space bar
To select an entire column	Control + space bar
To select the whole worksheet	Control + shift + space bar
To extend your selection up, down, right, or left	Shift + directional cursor key
The toggle key for extending a selection	F8
To activate the formula bar	F2
To calculate documents	F9

Moving around a dialog box

Action	Key
To move to the following option button group, command button, list, text, or check box	Tab
To move to and/or select in an active group of option buttons	Directional cursor keys
To turn on or off an active check box or choose the active command button	Space bar
To move to an item in a list box and select it	The key corresponding to the first letter of the item
To exit a dialog box	Escape to cancel; Enter to accept new options and exit

Using a Mouse in *Excel*

Action	Mouse Action
To move the window	Drag the title bar.
To close the window	Double-click the Control menu icon.
To scroll the window	Click horizontal or vertical scroll arrows.
To speed up scrolling	Drag the scroll box.
To scroll to a general location	Drag the scroll box in the scroll bar to the approximate desired location in your document; if you want to enter information or edit near the end, drag the scroll box to the end of the scroll bar, and so forth.
To maximize, minimize, or restore the window	Click on arrows in the upper right-hand corner of the screen.
To split the window into panes	Drag the split bar at the lower left-hand corner of the screen.
To enter or cancel current contents of formula bar	Click on the check mark (to enter) or on the X (to cancel) at the top left of the screen.

Selecting Cells

Undoubtedly the most basic and vital function of *Excel* is the process of selecting cells. *Excel* must know which cells you want to work with before you can enter data into a cell or perform any other operation. You can select:

• One cell at a time

Or

• A range of cells

To select a single cell using the mouse:
• Point to the cell you wish to activate.
• Click the mouse.

To select a single cell using the keyboard:
• Press the appropriate direction keys until the desired cell is reached.

A black border appears around the cell indicating it is now the active cell in the worksheet. (This cell is also called the *highlighted* cell.) You can enter information into the cell, or use any of a multitude of commands to format, copy, delete, or otherwise manipulate it.

To select a cell range using the mouse:
• Point to the cell you want to define as the upper left corner of the range.
• Press the mouse button.
• Next, drag the mouse to the cell you want to define as the lower right corner of the range, and then release the button.

To select a cell range using the keyboard:
• Hold down the shift key while using the direction keys to extend the selection. The entire range is now highlighted with a black border.

To select large ranges of cells with the mouse by using the shift key rather than dragging:
• Select the cell you want to define as the upper left corner of the range.
• Hold down the shift key.
• Click the cell you want to define as the opposite corner of the range.

To select entire rows and columns of cells using the mouse:
• Click in the appropriate row or column header.

To select entire rows and columns of cells using the keyboard:
• Hold down the shift key.
• Press the space bar to select an entire row holding the active cell(s), and use the Control key with the space bar to select

Using Excel

89

an entire column. The first cell of the selected row or column then becomes the active cell.

It is also possible to select more than one adjacent row or column at a time by dragging through all the corresponding row or column headers. Or, with the keyboard, select cells from entire rows/columns you want selected; then use shift or Control with the space bar as described above.

A single range can consist of several different areas. These are called multiple-area ranges or discontinuous ranges. Any combination of cells can encompass a discontinuous range.

To select multiple ranges with a mouse:
• Drag through the first area of cells.
• Press the Control key.
• Drag through the next area of cells.
    When you have dragged through the last area you wish to select, while continuing to hold down the Control key, click the last cell you wish to include.

To select multiple ranges with the keyboard:
• Select the first cell.
• Hold down the shift key and extend the selection.
• Then press F8 (with shift still pressed) to turn on Add.
• Now move to the next area with the direction keys, and se-
  lect it by holding down the shift key. Repeat the process until
  all the areas you want are selected. An alternative to shifting
  to extend a selection is to press F8 to turn on Extend.

Cell Entries

Once you have selected a cell you can begin entering information into it. There are two types of cell entries, *constant values* and *formulas*. Constant values consist of text, numeric
values, and date/time values.

Text entries vs. numeric entries. A text entry is basically
any entry that cannot be interpreted as a number, whereas a
number entry is any entry that only includes numerals from
the range 0–9. However, certain symbols such as the dollar
sign, percent sign, and comma are classified as numeric
entries.

It is important to know the distinction between text and numeric entries. *Excel* allows you to create formulas that link text cells to text cells or number cells to number cells, but you cannot mix the two. If you attempt to link a text cell to a number cell you will get a #VALUE! error.

Entering text is nearly the same as entering a number—select the cell and type in the entry. You then lock the entry just as you would with a number entry.

If you have an entry such as *216 Maple St.*, it is a little more difficult to differentiate between the two. An easy way to see how *Excel* would classify this is to see how it is aligned. *Excel* always aligns numeric entries to the right side of the cell and text entries to the left. If you enter *216 Maple St.* into a cell, you will notice that it is aligned to the left, indicating that it is a text entry.

There may be certain instances where you want *Excel* to classify an entry consisting of numbers as a text entry. This can be accomplished by simply putting quotation marks around the number. For example, "239" would be classified as text. The quotation marks indicate it is a text string rather than a numerical one.

Unlike number entries, long text entries may extend into adjacent cells. However, this is only for display purposes. In actuality the text is only taking up one cell.

Formulas. Formulas can be used with text data or numerical data. You can use a formula to combine text strings from two different cells or numerical strings from two different cells. Formula entries are always preceded by an equals sign (=).

For example, if cell A1 contains the text string SALARIES and cell A2 contains the text string EMPLOYEE BENEFITS, you can combine the two by entering the formula =A1& " and " &A2 into cell A3. The combined string is then entered in cell A3 as SALARIES and EMPLOYEE BENEFITS. Note the spaces before and after the word in quotation marks: " and ".

To enter a constant or a formula in your worksheet, select a cell and type in what you wish to enter. The entry then appears in the formula bar as well as in the active cell.

After you have made the entry, you need to lock it in in order to permanently store it in the cell. To do this, press the

Enter key. If you wish to delete what you have just entered, press the Escape key.

As you type in an entry, an Entry box and Cancel box appear in the formula bar. If you have a mouse, the Entry box is another way of locking in your entry. You simply click the Entry box rather than pressing the Enter key. The Cancel box gives you the option of deleting the information you just typed.

There is another process that locks in an entry while simultaneously activating an adjacent cell. You can make use of this by pressing Tab, Shift-Tab, or any of the direction keys, rather than Enter. Pressing Tab activates the cell directly to the right of the entry you lock in, while pressing Shift-Tab activates the cell directly to the left of the cell you just locked in. Pressing any of the direction keys activates the appropriate adjacent cell.

You may want to create a formula to total an expense column on your worksheet. Let's suppose you wanted to total cells B1–B3 and put the total in B5. To do this:
• You first select B5 and = .
• Then click B3 and enter + .
• Then select B2 and enter another + sign.
• Select B1.
• Finally, press Enter.

The formula bar shows the formula and B5 shows the total value of cells B1–B3. If you later change the value of cell B1, B2, or B3, *Excel* automatically adjusts the value in cell B5.

More on Numeric Entries

You can begin number entries with a plus (+) or minus (−) sign to designate the entry as positive or negative. If you enter a minus sign, *Excel* retains it. If you enter a plus sign, it is dropped, although the number is still interpreted as positive.

Numbers enclosed in parentheses are also considered negative. Therefore, the entry (200) would be interpreted as −200.

Entries preceded by a dollar sign ($) are interpreted as currency values and *Excel* automatically puts commas in the appropriate places. Conversely, commas entered in numbers that are not designated as currencies are removed by *Excel*.

Numbers can be entered in scientific notation with the characters *E* and *e*. For instance, if you make the entry 1E4, *Excel* interprets it as 10,000 (or 1 times 10 to the fourth power). If you enter a number that is too long for the width of the cell, *Excel* automatically converts it to scientific notation for you. If you look in the formula bar you will see the number displayed just as you entered it. The reason for this is that the actual contents of the cell are just as you entered them. However, the appearance has been changed in order to keep the number from overlapping into the next cell.

Date and Time Entries

Dates and times are stored as serial numbers. A serial number is a number between 0 and 65380. The number 1 represents the date January 1, 1900 and 65380 represents the date December 31, 2078.

Dates can be entered in these formats:

Format	Displayed As
m/d/yy	9/10/87
d-mmm-yy	10-Sep-87
d-mmm	10-Sep
mmm-yy	Sep-87
m/d/yy h:mm	9/10/87 20:50

If a cell has not been formatted *Excel* automatically uses m/d/yy as the General format. However, if you enter m/d/yy into a cell that has been formatted differently, *Excel* converts it to the format of the cell. For example, if you type 10-Sep into a cell that has the d-mmm-yy format, *Excel* displays it as 10-Sep-87.

Regardless of how the cell is formatted, you can use hyphens or slashes, and upper- or lowercase letters, when entering dates.

Times are stored by assigning each second in the day a fractional serial number. Each decimal fraction represents how much time has passed since midnight. 12:00:00 AM is represented by 0, 0.5 is used for 12:00:00 PM, and 0.99999 is the number directly before 12:00:00 AM.

Times can be entered in any of five formats:

Format	Displayed As
h:mm AM/PM	3:45 PM
h:mm:ss AM/PM	3:45:09 PM
h:mm	15:45
h:mm:ss	15:45:09
m/d/yy h:mm	9/10/87 15:45

When entering any of these formats you can use *A* or *P* instead of AM and PM and you can use upper- or lowercase letters.

It is possible to enter both a time and date into a cell; simply leave a space between the two entries.

If you want to format a date or time using a format other than one of the above, you can define your own using the number command from the Format menu.

Formula Entries

One of *Excel*'s most important features is its ability to calculate new values from existing ones. You simply enter the formula, and *Excel* does the calculating. Formulas can consist of *operators* or *functions*.

An operator is a mathematical sign that instructs *Excel* to calculate a new value from existing values. For example, in the formula $=7-2$, the minus sign $(-)$ is the operator that instructs *Excel* to subtract 2 from 7 and produce the value 5. The numbers 7 and 2 are considered the *operands*.

It is also possible for a formula to have only one operand. For instance, in the formula $=5\%$, the percent sign instructs *Excel* to divide the operand (in this case, 5) by 100 to produce the value 0.05.

There are four types of operators:
• Arithmetic
• Text
• Comparison
• Reference

The arithmetic operators calculate basic math equations. Existing values can be added, subtracted, multiplied, or divided by one another to produce new values which are then displayed in the cell with the formula.

There are seven arithmetic operators:

Operator	Meaning
+	Add
−	Subtract
−	Negate (used with one operand)
*	Multiply
/	Divide
%	Percent (divide by 100)
^	Raise to an exponent

It is important to know the order in which *Excel* performs these operations in complex formulas. If a formula has more than one operand, *Excel* calculates operations in parentheses first, then multiplication and division, and finally, addition and subtraction.

For example, in the formula $=8+10/2$, *Excel* first divides 2 into 10, then adds the product to 8 to produce a value of 13. If you want to have the product of 8 and 10 divided by 2, you need to add parentheses: $(8+10)/2$. The resulting value is then 9. In the event of two operations of the same level, *Excel* calculates them from left to right.

There is only one text operator, the ampersand (&). It is used to join two or more text values. For example, the formula =''Mrs.'' & ''Smith'' produces Mrs. Smith as the new text value.

A comparison operator is used to compare two values and produce a logical True or False value. For instance, the value *expenses>1000* produces the value True if the value of expenses is more than 1000, and a False if it is less than or equal to 1000.

There are six comparison operators:

Operator	Meaning
=	Equals
< >	Not equal to
>	Greater than
<	Less than
>=	Greater than or equal to
<=	Less than or equal to

A reference describes the location of a cell or range of cells with a sequence of characters. You can use references in formulas to link the formula to other cells in your worksheet.

The value of the formula then reflects the value of the cells. For example, say you selected cell A15 and entered the formula =A10+A11−A12*A13. Now let's suppose these cells had the following entries: A10 (50), A11 (20), A12 (10), and A13 (2). *Excel* would calculate these values using the formula and display the resulting value of 50 in cell A15. If later you were to change the entry in cell A10 to 40, *Excel* would automatically change the entry in cell A15 to reflect the new value of 40.

A reference operator consolidates two references into one new reference. There are three reference operators:
• Range
• Union
• Intersection

Range reference operator. A range reference operator produces one reference for all cells between the two references. It is designated by a colon (:). For example, to refer to all of column A you would type A:A, or to refer to all of rows 1–5 you would type 1:5.

Union reference operator. A union reference operator combines the two references into one reference. It is designated by a comma (,). For example, if you wanted one reference to include cells B3 and C2, you would enter B3,C2.

Intersection reference operator. The intersection reference operator takes the cells common to the two references and produces one. This operator is specified by entering a space between the column and row reference. For instance, if

you wanted one reference to designate the intersection between column C and row 4, you would enter C 4.

It is important to know the order in which *Excel* performs
operations in the event that a formula consists of more than
one operation. The order is as follows:
- Range (:)
- Intersection ( )
- Union (,)
- Negation (−)
- Percent (%)
- Exponentiation (^)
- Multiplication and division (* and /)
- Addition and subtraction (+ and −)
- Text operator (&)
- Comparison operators (=, <, <=, >, >=, and <>)

Circular references. When two or more cells are dependent on each other, *Excel* is unable to resolve the formula in
either cell. For example, if you enter the formula =D2−A2 in
cell A2, *Excel* responds with the alert message CAN'T RE-
SOLVE CIRCULAR REFERENCES. You then need to click OK
to acknowledge the error, in which case the formula displays
the value 0.

Excel is unable to solve the above formula because each
time it derives a value for the formula in cell A2, the value of
the cell changes. It then evaluates the formula in A2 using the
new value, causing the value in A2 to change once again. This
circle goes on indefinitely with no possibility of producing a
resolution.

However, there are some circular references that can be
resolved with the use of iteration. When *Excel* uses iteration,
formulas are calculated over and over using the results of the
previous calculation.

To use this feature, click OK after the CAN'T RESOLVE
CIRCULAR REFERENCES message appears. Then select the
Calculation command from the Options menu. A dialog box
appears. Click the Manual and Iteration boxes and then enter
the maximum number of iterations you want performed or the
maximum change in value you want reached. *Excel* will stop

Using Excel

when it arrives at one of these limits.

If you don't specify limitations, *Excel* performs 100 iterations or continues until all values change by less than 0.001 between iterations.

A circular reference is beneficial in many business calculations. For example, it could be used to calculate a commission that was based on 5 percent of net profit, whereby the net profit would be figured by subtracting the bonus from the gross profit. If you knew the value for the gross profit, but not for the net profit or the bonus, you would have a circular reference. Since the bonus was 5 percent of the net profit, you'd need to know the value of the net profit before you could calculate the bonus. However, you could not figure out the net profit unless you knew the bonus. In this case you would need a circular reference to propose a resolution.

Formatting Cells

Unless you specify otherwise, *Excel* inputs all entries in the General format. The most obvious characteristic of this format is the method of aligning numbers to the right and text to the left.

With the use of *Excel*'s formatting commands you can change the format, alignment, and style of your worksheet entries rather than using the General format. These commands are beneficial for such things as enhancing certain entries with boldface letters or darkened underlining. This makes reading a worksheet easier, as the entries in an unformatted worksheet tend to blend together, making it difficult to interpret.

Not surprisingly, most of *Excel*'s formatting commands are located on the Format menu. These include:
• Number
• Alignment
• Font
• Border
• Column width

Other important formatting commands are located on the Options menu. These are:
• Display and Workspace commands. The following chart

shows what effect various formatting commands have on a numeric entry.

If you enter 12345.678 into a cell:

Formatted as	It is displayed as	Comments
General	12345.678	
0	12346	Rounds off last place
0.00	12345.68	Rounds off to two decimal places
#,##0	12,346	Displays commas
#,##0.00	12,345.68	Displays commas and two decimal places
$#,##0;(#,##0)	$12,346	Displays negative numbers in parentheses
$#,##0.00;(#,##0.00)	$12,346.68	Displays negative numbers in parentheses
0%	1234568%	Moves decimal two places to the right
0.00%	1234567.80%	Moves decimal two places to the right and displays two decimal places
0.00E+00	1.23E+04	Exponential format

How to format cells. Formatting a cell or range of cells is not difficult to do. Begin by selecting the cells you want to format. This can be a single cell, a range of cells, or the entire worksheet. You can make your cell entries and then format the cell, or format an empty cell and then make the entries. It is easiest, however, to select a range of cells, make the cell entries, and then while the range is still selected, choose a format.

Let's suppose you are formatting an Operating Expenses Worksheet in this sequence. You have made all the entries and now you want to round each value in the expense column to two decimal places.

• First, select the cells you wish to format.
• Then choose the Number command from the Format menu.
• Select the 0.00 option in the dialog box.

Now suppose you want these numbers displayed in bold type:
• Simply choose the Font command.
• Select a bold font.

A cell will remain formatted even if you change its contents. For example, suppose after formatting a cell in the above example, you realize that you've made a mistake in one of the entries. To correct it, click the cell with the error, type in the correct number, and then click the OK button. The new number appears with two decimal places, just as the cell was originally formatted.

It's also possible to erase the contents of a cell without disturbing the format. To do this:
• Select the cells in question.
• Choose the Clear command from the Edit menu.
• Select the Formulas option, and the contents of the cell will be eliminated.

Any new entries made in this cell will automatically be adjusted to fit the format of the cell. Nearly the same procedure is used to delete the format of a cell:
• Select the cell or range of cells.
• Select the Clear command from the Edit menu.
• In the dialog box that appears select the Formats option.
This eliminates the format of the cell, but does not affect the contents.

To delete the contents as well as the format:
• Choose the All option in the dialog box.

Excel is unique in that it allows you to create your own numeric formats. You can either modify an existing format or create an entirely new one. The following chart explains the symbols to use when creating your own format.

Symbol	Meaning
General	Use the default format.
0	Digit place holder. If the number of zeros on either side of the decimal point exceeds the number of digits on either side of the decimal point, the zeros will be shown. But, if the number of digits on the right (in the actual number) exceeds the number of zeros on the right (in the format), the number is rounded, leaving as many decimal places as there are zeros.
#	This symbol serves as a place holder. It follows the same rules as the zero above, except that zeros are not displayed if the number of place holders exceeds the number of digits on either side of the decimal.
.	The decimal point format determines how many digits are displayed on either side of the decimal point. The default is to display numbers between −1 and 1 with a leading decimal point; the convention is to provide a leading zero to the left of the decimal point. A person scanning a report might accidentally read .1234 as 1234, but few people would mistakenly read 0.1234, because whole numbers do not begin with leading zeros. To obtain this feature, format the cell with a leading zero rather than a leading place holder.

Symbol	Meaning
%	Using the percent symbol results in an automatic shift of the decimal point two digits to the right, along with the insertion of the percent symbol.
,	In all cases except years A.D. or B.C., numbers greater than 999 are broken into powers of 1000. The reason for this is obvious: It takes a certain amount of calculation to figure out what the number 10000000 represents. The number 10,000,000 is much clearer. Commas are inserted if this format is chosen.
E− E+ e− e+	Including these symbols in the format to the left of a zero or a place holder provides for scientific notation. The minus sign provides for a minus sign in the case of negative exponents. Use of the plus sign provides for a sign designation whether the exponent is positive or negative.
:, $, −, +, (,), and the space character	Use of these symbols allows *Excel* to use the symbol in the formatted value. You may want to use other characters. This is accomplished simply by enclosing the needed symbol in its designated place (within the string of zeros, place holders, and so on) with a quotation mark on either side of it or so that it is preceded by a backslash (see below).
\	This symbol tells the program to include the following symbol in the formatted display. The backslash itself will not appear.
*	The asterisk informs *Excel* that the next character should be repeated enough times to fill the width of the column.
"Text"	Placing text (or any symbol) within quotation marks will result in its being placed within the formatted number. The quotation marks will not appear.

To create your own format:
- Select the cells you wish to format.
- Choose the Number command from the Format menu. A dialog box appears with a list of proposed formats.
- Type over a format with your own, and then click the OK button.

The formats you create are then added to the list and from then on appear as options whenever you click the Number command. As an example of how this works, if you want to create a social security number format, you type ###-##-#### in the dialog box. After the cell is formatted, you enter a number such as 563994567. It is then displayed as 563-99-4567.

To delete a format you have created:
- Click the format from the dialog box.
- Click the Delete button. You can only delete from this list formats that you created; you cannot delete an *Excel* format.

Another part of the the General format you may wish to modify is the order in which the text and numbers are formatted. As mentioned earlier, the General format aligns numeric entries to the right and text entries to the left.

To change this order:
- Choose the Alignment command from the Format menu. A dialog box appears with four other options: Left, Center, Right, and Fill.
The *Left* option aligns the contents of the cell to the left. This option can be used to align numbers to the left rather than letting them default to the right.
The *Center* option centers all entries.
The *Right* option aligns everything to the right.
The *Fill* option tells *Excel* to repeat the contents of the cell until the entire cell is filled.

The Alignment command affects long text entries that don't fit in a single cell. With the General alignment, long entries overflow into adjoining cells on the right. If you use the Center option to align a cell, text that doesn't fit overflows into both the right *and* left adjoining cells. If these cells already contain entries, the text is still centered, but the first few characters are not visible. If you align text to the right, it only overflows into the left adjoining cell. Conversely, if you align text to the left, it overflows into the right adjoining cell. This feature allows you considerable flexibility in the display of your worksheet.

The Fill option tells *Excel* to repeat the contents of the cell until the entire cell is filled. For example, on an Operating Expenses Worksheet, you might want to separate a column of figures from the total with a line of dashes. To do this, type a single dash in the designated cell, select the Alignment command, and then click the Fill option.

It may seem just as easy to simply type the dashes across the cell manually. The Fill option has an important advantage, however. If you were to subsequently increase the width of the cell, *Excel* would automatically expand the dashes to fit the width, relieving you of the burden of making the adjustment.

Fonts command. The Fonts command also allows you to change the display of your worksheet. This command gives you the options of various fonts, along with Bold or Italic type.

- Simply select the cell whose style you wish to change.
- Choose the Fonts command.
- Select among the fonts and options.

These formatting commands all affect the appearance of individual cells, whereas the formatting commands from the Options menu affect the appearance of the overall worksheet—most notably the Display and Workspace commands.

The Display command enables you to alter the display of formulas, gridlines, and row and column headings.

Formulas. The Formulas option enables you to view all the underlying values and formulas of your worksheet simultaneously. To do this, choose the Display command, then the Formulas option, and then the OK button. As a result, the actual formulas and underlying values will be shown instead of the usual display, which only shows the results of the formulas or the value formats.

This option is of immense benefit in editing a large worksheet. For instance, if you had an error in a formula that was linked to several other formulas, you would have to choose each cell connected to the formula to see the underlying value in the formula bar and locate the error.

All of the columns in the worksheet will automatically expand to twice their normal width, plus one character. For example, a column that normally has four characters will become nine characters wide.

Gridlines. In the General format, dotted gridlines designate the boundaries of each cell. Although this can be beneficial, there are times you may not want them. To eliminate gridlines, select the Display command and then unchoose the Gridlines option.

Row and Column Headings. The Row and Column Headings option eliminates the numbers normally displayed on the left of the worksheet to indicate row numbers, and the letters at the top of the worksheet that represent individual columns. You simply choose this option and then click the OK button.

While row and column headers are beneficial in creating and interpreting your worksheet, in some instances you may want to eliminate them for display purposes.

As with other Display options, the Row and Column Headings only apply to the worksheet you are working on. If you have more than one open worksheet when you use this command, the row and column headers will only disappear from the active worksheet.

Chapter 3
Power User Tips

Chapter 3
Power User Tips

After you've familiarized yourself with *Excel*'s basic operating procedures, you are ready to take on some of the more advanced features. *Excel* has remarkable flexibility—this becomes all the more apparent as you examine the built-in features that set the program apart from its competition.

This chapter begins with a look at *functions,* which are basically shortcuts. Functions spare you a great deal of tedious typing, and occasionally, some outright difficult mathematical calculations. Other functions perform specialized tasks which are more logical than mathematical.

Next the chapter turns to *macros,* which take the concept of a function one step further. Macros allow you to design your own functions. These can be convenient when *Excel* doesn't have a built-in function to suit your needs. Another kind of macro is actually a program. If you find yourself typing in the same commands over and over, a command macro can save you the trouble.

Finally, there's a look at *arrays,* which allow you to perform a mathematical operation on a group of numbers simultaneously, yielding a group of answers.

When you have mastered the concepts in this chapter, you will truly be getting the most from *Excel.*

Functions

Most functions are built-in formulas. Their purpose is simply to save you the trouble of concocting and typing in a commonly used formula. Other functions, such as IF, have special uses and are unlike formulas.

If you wanted to find the sum of cells A1:A8, you could enter the formula

$$=A1+A2+A3+A4+A5+A6+A7+A8$$

or you could use *Excel*'s built-in function: $=SUM(A1:A8)$. The purpose of a function is to keep you from the tedious and often difficult job of figuring out and entering a formula. It's a shortcut.

Excel's built-in functions fall into categories:

- The *statistical functions* deal with lists of numbers—you can sum them, average them, find the highest or lowest, count them, and manipulate them with other, more advanced functions that require an understanding of statistics to use.
- The *mathematical functions* perform operations such as finding the absolute value, sign, and square root of a number, rounding off or converting a number into an integer, or generating a random number.
- The *financial functions* can analyze an investment by finding such things as present value, future value, interest rate, and number of periods.
- In addition, there are *logarithmic, trigonometric, text,* and *logical* functions.

A function, like a formula, must always begin with an equals sign (=), which keeps it from being misinterpreted as text. Most functions take *arguments,* which are the parameters enclosed in parentheses and separated by commas. An argument is usually a cell reference, but it can also be a constant, an array, a cell range reference, or another function which is nested inside the outer function.

Macros

Macros fall into two categories:

- A *function macro* allows you to make your own, "user-defined," functions. Once you have created a function macro, you merely type in its name and leave the rest of the work to *Excel.* (These are not to be confused with *macro functions,* which are built-in functions that can be used only in macros.) A function macro does not perform actions, but performs calculations.
- A *command macro* is a list of commands that you create. It's very similar to a program. When you run the macro, *Excel* executes the commands (a planned sequence of actions such as entering data or selecting cells) in order.

If *Excel* does not have a particular built-in function that you need, you can create one by making a function macro. A command macro, on the other hand, is a way to act on the worksheet by stringing together commands. You may be familiar with the term *batching* as it applies to operating system commands; a command macro batches *Excel* commands.

Macros can be as complex or as simple as you desire. On the complex side, macros can be hundreds of entries long. *Excel*'s macro language contains over 125 different functions which can be used with macros. In other words, to get the full power of *Excel*'s macros requires a commitment similar to learning a programming language.

On the other hand, most users of *Excel* are not interested in becoming programmers. You probably just want to use *Excel* for specific business applications. This lesson is aimed at the applications user, not the programmer. (For those who want to delve into the subject in greater detail, however, we can highly recommend *The Complete Book of Excel Macros*, Louis Benjamin and Don Nicholas, published by Osborne/McGraw-Hill, 1986.)

To create a macro you need two sheets:
• A standard worksheet
• A macro sheet

To open a macro sheet:
• Drag down the File menu to the New command.
• Select Macro Sheet.
• Position the macro sheet so that you can switch back and forth between it and the worksheet.

A macro will act on your worksheet. However, you need a place where the macro's commands can go. That is the purpose of a macro sheet. It's like a note pad that keeps the macro's instructions.

One way to approach a command macro is to enter commands directly on the macro sheet, then run it. As you get more sophisticated, you may very well want to do this. However, *Excel* provides an easier way to program the macro sheet. It's called a *recorder*.

The recorder. With the recorder you simply enter commands on the worksheet as you would if you were altering the worksheet. Your every keystroke and mouse movement is recorded and listed on the macro sheet. That sequence of commands becomes instantly available whenever you want to repeat it by running it.

Creating a macro. In this case actually writing a macro is worth a thousand words in description. So let's get started.

• Activate the macro sheet.

Make the macro sheet active by selecting it. Now dedicate a range for our new macro. The easiest way to do this is to highlight a column. We'll pick column A—just click the *A* at the top of the column if you're using a mouse, or put the cursor in cell A1 and press Ctrl + Space bar if you're using the keyboard.

• Set the recorder.

We now need to tell *Excel* that we are going to be using the highlighted column to enter a macro. We do this by dragging down from the Macro menu to Set Recorder. When we click the mouse (or choose this command) nothing discernible happens. Yet, rest assured, *Excel* now knows that we mean the A column to be the area where the macro formulas will go.

• Pick the starting cell.

Make the worksheet active again. Pick the cell where you want to start recording macro formulas. We'll select cell A1.

• Cell A1 needs to be a bit wider to accommodate our macro lines. Press Alt-T-C to choose the Column Width command and type 25 in the text box. Press Enter.

• Turn on the recorder. Drag down Macro to Start Recorder. Again, nothing discernible happens. However, as long as the recorder is on, every keystroke or mouse stroke we enter will automatically be transferred as a command from the worksheet to the macro sheet.

• Begin programming.

Now we just key or mouse in whatever we want the macro to do.

At this point, let's actually try creating a macro that we can use later on. If you haven't done so already, complete all the steps detailed above. Now to begin:
• Type your own name in cell A1 and press Enter.
• Type your address and press Enter again.
• Type your city, state, and zip, and press Enter again.
• Finally, enter the current date/time function =NOW( ).
• Press Enter.

Your worksheet should look similar to Figure 3-1.

Figure 3-1. Your Worksheet Should Look Similar to This

	A
1	Fred Jones
2	4321 Orange St.
3	Los Angeles CA 90046
4	32157.71281

Let's clean up what we've written:
• With cell A4 (the date/time cell) still active, pull down Format to Number and choose the last selection (m/d/yy h:mm). Immediately *Excel* will change its code number to the current date and time.
• Now, highlight all four cells and pull down Format to Alignment.
• Select Center. All of your text should be centered in the cells.
• Finally, pull down Format to Fonts and select the bold font. All of the text should now be in boldface.
• Make cell A5 (the one directly below the text) active. Your worksheet should look like Figure 3-2.

Figure 3-2. Your Formatted Worksheet

	A
1	Fred Jones
2	4321 Orange St.
3	Los Angeles CA 90046
4	1/15/88 17:06

Congratulations! You've completed your first macro. Now you need to complete the steps to make the macro ready to run.

• Turn off the recorder.

Remember, everything you've keyed or moused in thus far has been recorded on the macro sheet. Since you've stopped programming, it's time to stop the recorder. Just choose Stop Recorder from the Macro menu.

• Name the macro.

In order to run a macro, it's first necessary to name it. This is easily done. Make the macro sheet active now. The range you originally defined should look like Figure 3-3.

Figure 3-3. Originally Defined Macro Range

	A
1	Name
2	=FORMULA("Fred Jones")
3	=SELECT("R2C1")
4	=FORMULA("4321 Orange St.")
5	=SELECT("R3C1")
6	=FORMULA("Los Angeles CA 90046")
7	=SELECT("R4C1")
8	=FORMULA("=NOW()")
9	=FORMAT.NUMBER("m/d/yy h:mm")
10	=SELECT("R1C1:R4C1")
11	=ALIGNMENT(3)
12	=FORMAT.FONT("Helv",10,TRUE,FALSE,FALSE,FALSE)
13	=SELECT("R5C1")
14	=RETURN()

Before naming the macro, take a close look at it. Notice that all of the cells are formulas (they all start with an equals sign). In addition, if you look carefully you'll realize that you can actually read the macro. Can you see where you've typed in your name, address, and so forth? *Excel* automatically selected the macro function FORMULA( ) to put these in. It also used the macro functions SELECT( ) and menu commands ALIGNMENT( ), FORMAT.NUMBER( ) and STYLE( ).

Naming the macro is easy:
- First, insert an empty cell at the top.
- Now make the cell you just inserted active.
- Type in *NAME* (you can call it whatever you'd like) and press Enter.
- Now drag down Formula to Define Name. You'll see that your entry, *NAME*, is already suggested. But before okaying it, click Command at the bottom of the box. This tells *Excel* that the macro will be activated by a command from you.

You also have the option of using a special key to activate the macro.
- Type in *N* in the Key box. (We'll see how this works shortly.)

Now your macro is done. When you'd like your name to appear on a worksheet, just run this macro and what you've typed will instantly be reproduced there.

Try it now.
- Run the macro.

Return to the worksheet and activate cell C1 (the first words of your macro will appear in whatever cell you make active). Now drag down from Macro to Run. A box appears, listing the various macros available. Just select *NAME* and immediately *Excel* creates your name, address, and the current date and time. It then centers all entries and puts them in boldface. Finally, it makes the cell directly under the last entry the active one.

You can save this macro and use it whenever you start up a new worksheet. A quick way to call up this macro (instead of using the Macro, Run, and *NAME* commands) is to hold down the Option and Command keys while typing *N* (for *Name*, which you entered as an option key). The macro immediately executes, beginning wherever you've placed the active cell. (Did you remember to use a capital *N* ?)

Once you've created a macro, it can be altered to do almost anything you like.

To change the macro:
- Simply make the macro sheet active.
- Now edit it as you would any other worksheet.

Interactive macros. It is possible to create macros that interact with the user. This means that instead of executing the entire macro, *Excel* pauses at a designated spot and asks the user to input information in a special input box.

You can use the function INPUT in your macro to accomplish this. It's important, however, to use the correct form:

INPUT(*prompt,type,title*)

Prompt stands for whatever message you want displayed. *Type* stands for the kind of return desired. *Excel* offers seven alternatives:

Type	Meaning
0	Returns a formula
1	Returns a number
2	Returns text
4	Logical Return
8	Returns a reference
16	Returns an error
64	Returns an array

Title stands for the desired action.

An example would be

=INPUT("Enter 'yes' or 'no' ",2,"Select")

Another method of inputting would be to use existing dialog boxes. Many of *Excel*'s macro functions correspond to worksheet menus. Those that do correspond have a question mark (?) after them, such as DEFINE.NAME?( ). Using these macros with the question mark interrupts the macro and calls up the dialog box.

Function macros. Function macros are used as part of a formula. Instead of having a command to call them up, they are activated by the formula itself. This shouldn't be a difficult concept to grasp. You already know what functions are and what macros are. Put them together and you get macros that act like functions, or *function macros*.

The rules for function macros are somewhat different from those for command macros. For one thing, you can't use the recorder to create them. Instead, they must be written directly onto a macro sheet.

Also, naming function macros is different from naming command macros. When naming a function macro, we check the function target in the Define Name box. The procedure goes like this:
• Create the macro.
• Activate the first cell.
• Drag down from Formula to Define Name and give it a name (the name is normally already in the first cell).
• Select Macro Function instead of Macro Command and press Enter.

The most important difference between command macros and function macros has to do with arguments. A function macro works just like a function. It is composed of three parts:
• Arguments
• Instructions on what to do with the arguments
• Instructions on what to do with the result

Figure 3-4 shows a simple function macro that illustrates this difference.

Figure 3-4. A Function Macro

	A	B
1	COMMISSION	Names the macro
2	=ARGUMENT("SALES")	Names the first argument
3	=ARGUMENT("COMMISSION")	Names the second argument
4	=SALES/COMMISSION	Divides the first argument by the second argument
5	=RETURN(A4)	Stops macro/produces the result of cell A4

As usual, the first row gives the macro a name for easy identification. The next two rows are like the names of two arguments in a function. Cells A2 and A3 tell *Excel* what the arguments are called.

Next, we tell *Excel* what to do with the two arguments—in this case, simply divide.

Finally, we need to tell the program what to do with the result of the division and to stop the macro. Line 5A does this.

This simple function macro will calculate commissions for us. To use it we need a worksheet.

Figure 3-5. Commission Worksheet

	A	B	C	D
1	Salesperson	Sales	Commission	
2	Henry	10000	=FUNCTIONMACRO!$A$1(B2,10)	1000
3	Helen	12000	=FUNCTIONMACRO!$A$1(B3,10)	1200
4	Dorothy	14000	=FUNCTIONMACRO!$A$1(B4,10)	1400
5				
6				
7	Bill	15000	=FUNCTIONMACRO!$A$1(B7,10)	1250
8	Sarah	12000	=FUNCTIONMACRO!$A$1(B8,10)	1000

We call up a function macro just as we would any other macro:

- On the worksheet, begin with the formula equals sign (=).
- Next indicate the function macro we want to run. It can be typed in; however, since we'd have to type both the macro sheet and the macro name, it's easier simply to type an equals sign (=), then activate the macro sheet and click on the name of the macro. Instantly it will be copied to the formula line.
- Now create a parenthetical expression.

The first argument is for the sales amounts. We already have that in the column under sales. For Henry, therefore, all we need do is refer to cell B2. For the commission, we currently are calculating that each salesperson gets 1/10th of sales, so we put in 10. (If the salesperson got 1/12th of sales, we would put in 12, and so forth. On the other hand, if we wanted to use a percentage, we could use 10 percent, but we would need to use multiplication instead of division in our macro to get the correct answer.)

- The formula using the macro function is complete. To run it, all you need do is type Enter. The calculation will immediately be made.

The remaining calculations on the sheet are far easier to make. We simply highlight the formula cell C2:C5 and use Fill Down from the Edit menu to place the formula in the remaining cells. They quickly fill in and our job is done.

Note: For purposes of clarity, the above illustration shows both the formulas and the results. Normally only one or the other would be displayed.

This was a simple example, but function macros can be quite long and complex. Any problem that can be solved by a mathematical formula can be solved by a function macro.

Arrays

An array allows you to perform a mathematical operation on a group of values simultaneously. It produces a group of results (an array of results).

Suppose we want to subtract the value in cell B1 from the value in cell A1. We can create a simple formula to accomplish this:

$$=A1-B1$$

But now suppose that we have a whole column of values in A and a whole column of values in B. We want to subtract all the values in A from all the values in column B. Then we want to know what the average of the result of all those calculations is.

We could, of course, use the formula described above to fill in column C, producing the results of subtracting the B's from the A's. Then we could add the result and divide by the total number to get the average. But *Excel's* array ability provides an easier way to do it.

In a single cell we can tell *Excel* to first subtract all of the B values from all of the corresponding A values, then average the result (see Figure 3-6).

Figure 3-6. Subtracting and Averaging Arrays

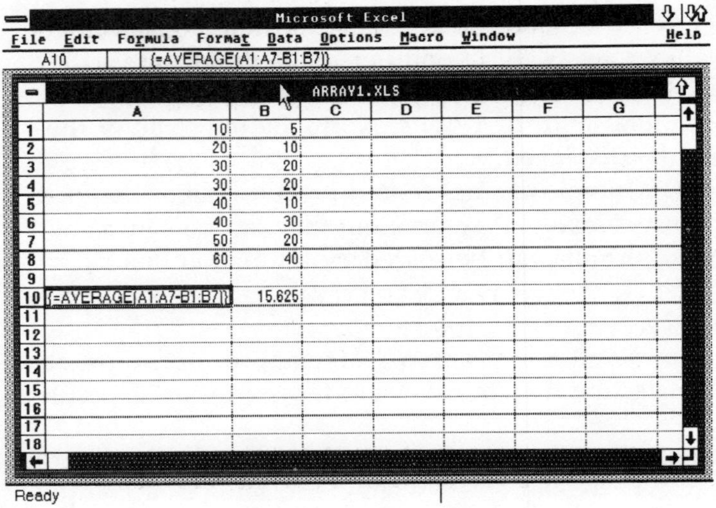

Notice that subtraction and averaging are accomplished in a single cell with a formula that looks like this:

$$\{=AVERAGE(A1:A7-B1:B7)\}$$

Let's take a closer look at this formula. The arguments tell *Excel* to consider the range of cells A1:A7 and the separate range of cells B1:B7. It then says to subtract the B range from the A range.

Most spreadsheets would show an error if you tried to do this. The reason is that most spreadsheets have no way of individually making the subtractions A1−B1, A2−B2, A3−B3, and so on, and then acting on them all from a single formula. To put it another way, the range A1:A7 is an array, a collection of individual values. The range B1:B7 is also an array. We are asking *Excel* to subtract the B array from the A array.

It should be clarified that, technically speaking, we aren't dealing with ranges, but with arrays. The difference is, in part, that *Excel* only recognizes arrays that are rectangular in shape (and ranges can be many different shapes, even discontinuous). {A1:B7} is considered a 1 × 7 array—one column by seven rows—not a range. {B1:B7} is a similar array.

Excel recognizes these kinds of arrays and deals with them appropriately. It individually subtracts the B's from the A's. Then, because we are using the AVERAGE function as part of our formula, it averages all the results and returns to us a single value. (For some functions, such as TREND, *Excel* can return an array.)

To indicate to *Excel* that a cell group should be defined as an array, hold the Control key down while pressing the Enter key. This tells *Excel* to recognize the reference as an array.

Notice that the formula for an array is surrounded by special braces: { }. When we key in an array, *Excel* acknowledges by putting those braces around the formula.

Let's look at another example in Figure 3-7.

Figure 3-7. Array Example

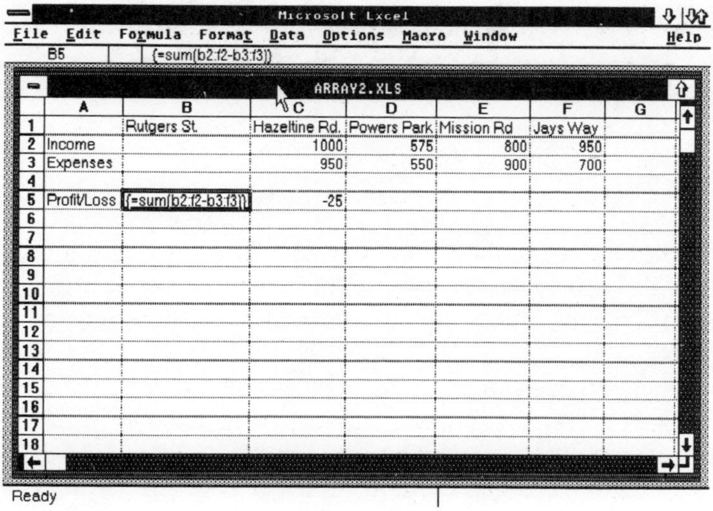

Here we have a number of rental homes identified by street. Each home produces income and has expenses. We want to know the bottom line. After all the expenses have been subtracted from all the incomes, is the owner making money or losing it?

This is accomplished simply with the array formula:

$$\{=SUM(B2:F2-B3:F3)\}$$

This formula tells *Excel* to subtract the B3:F3 array from the B2:F2 array, then add up the results and display it. Unfortunately, the results indicate that the owner is losing just a bit of money.

Array rules. In general, arrays don't require special rules, but there are exceptions. Once you've designated a rectangular area as an array, you can't change it in any way. You can't go into individual cells and add formulas, for example. This prevents *Excel* from carrying out its array function, and the program will tell you that you are conducting an illegal activity if you try it.

Also, when editing, remember to hold down the Control key after an edit, or else *Excel* will forget that it is dealing with an array.

Arrays are very useful tools. As with any new function, you must practice using them to become proficient with them. The time is well spent because you will find many uses for arrays once you become familiar with them.

Chapter 4
Ideas

Chapter 4
Ideas

This chapter contains easily created worksheet templates that perform various applications. The first section contains business operation templates. The next section contains real estate investment applications, with the final section covering database operations such as a mailing list.

Business Operations

Templates covered in this section include:
- Checkbook
- Ledger
- Cashflow
- Accounts receivable
- Sales

To use any of these applications in your business operations, simply follow the instructions for creating the model; then fill in the necessary data. It is not necessary to have read the previous chapters on *Excel* to construct working models. Reading through the explanatory chapters will, however, make the model construction easier.

Checkbook

Purpose. This model replaces a normal checkbook. It does all of the math and keeps a running balance, with a separate balance of all entries that have cleared the bank. The accompanying macro is used at the end of a period; it closes out the current checkbook and passes all totals and outstanding items to a new checkbook worksheet.

Figure 4-1. Checkbook Model

	A	B	C	D	E	F	G	H
1								
2					Running Balance:		$199.41	
3					Last Bank Balance:		$768.17	
4								
5					Opening Balance:		$343.54	
6								
7	Date	Ck#	Description	1/0	Amount	Deposit	Balance	Bank Bal.
8								
9	1-Jun	1091	Peachtree Associates	1	$200.00		$143.54	$143.54
10	8-Jun	1093	Jackson Enterprises	1	$50.00		$93.54	$93.54
11	10-Jun		Miller Publications	1		$750.50	$844.04	$844.04
12	12-Jun	1094	Dept. Water & Power	0	$28.16		$815.88	$844.04
13	12-Jun	1095	Edison	0	$45.60		$770.28	$844.04
14	12-Jun	1096	Pacific Bell	1	$75.87		$694.41	$768.17
15	15-Jun	1097	Eggwild Software	0	$495.00		$199.41	$768.17
16		1098					$199.41	$768.17
17		1099					$199.41	$768.17
18		1100					$199.41	$768.17
19		1101					$199.41	$768.17
20		1102					$199.41	$768.17
21		1103					$199.41	$768.17
22		1104					$199.41	$768.17
23		1105					$199.41	$768.17
24		1106					$199.41	$768.17
25		1107					$199.41	$768.17
26		1108					$199.41	$768.17
27		1109					$199.41	$768.17
28		1110					$199.41	$768.17

Constructing the model. To create your own checkbook spreadsheet:
• Open a new worksheet.
• Select all of column A by clicking the *A*.
• From the Format menu, select Column Width and enter 7.8.
• Click OK.

	A	B	C	D	E	F	G	H
29		1111					$199.41	$768.17
30		1112					$199.41	$768.17
31		1113					$199.41	$768.17
32		1114					$199.41	$768.17
33		1115					$199.41	$768.17
34		1116					$199.41	$768.17
35		1117					$199.41	$768.17
36		1118					$199.41	$768.17
37		1119					$199.41	$768.17
38		1120					$199.41	$768.17
39		1121					$199.41	$768.17
40		1122					$199.41	$768.17
41		1123					$199.41	$768.17
42		1124					$199.41	$768.17
43		1125					$199.41	$768.17
44		1126					$199.41	$768.17
45		1127					$199.41	$768.17
46		1128					$199.41	$768.17
47		1129					$199.41	$768.17
48		1130					$199.41	$768.17
49		1131					$199.41	$768.17
50		1132					$199.41	$768.17
51		1133					$199.41	$768.17
52		1134					$199.41	$768.17
53		1135					$199.41	$768.17
54		1136					$199.41	$768.17
55		1137					$199.41	$768.17
56		**CURRENT BALANCES**					$199.41	$768.17

You have just adjusted the width of column A. In the same manner, set the widths of the other columns as follows:

Column	Width
B	4
C	21.857
D	2.857
E	10
F	10
G	10
H	10

With the window set at its maximum size, these settings should allow columns A–G to be displayed in their entirety on the screen.

- From the Options menu, select Display.
- Remove the X from the Gridlines box, leaving an X only in the Row and Column Headings box.
- Click OK. The gridlines will clear from the screen.

Now you need to replace the grids you want.

- Select cells E2:F2.
- From the Format menu, select Border.
- Choose Outline, then OK. An outlined border will appear around E2:F2.
- Now select E3:F3 and put a border around these cells.
- Do the same for selections E5:F5, G2, G3, G5.
- Now select A7:H7 and check off every selection on the Border menu except Shading.
- Click OK.
- Now select A9:H56. An easy way to do this is to select A9 only, scroll to H56, then, while holding down the shift key, select H56. Or, you could select A9, use the Goto command on the Formula menu, type in H56 as the reference, and then, while holding down the shift key, press Enter. Check off every selection on the Border menu except Shading and click OK.
- Finally, select A56:F56, select Outline from the Border menu (you will have to uncheck the other selections), and click OK. This completes the grid layout.
- While you are down at row 56, select C56 and type in the text: CURRENT BALANCES.
- From the Format menu select Fonts and check off Bold. Also from the Format menu select Alignment and check off Center.
- Scroll back to the top of the worksheet and enter the remaining text as it is illustrated in Figure 4-1. Do not use the Checkbook Formula worksheet (Figure 4-2) for layout—it is not in proportion.

You'll be entering eleven more strings of text in the appropriate cells:
- Running Balance:
- Last Bank Balance:
- Opening Balance:
- Date
- Ck#
- Description
- 1/0
- Amount
- Deposit
- Balance
- Bank Bal.

These can all be boldfaced simultaneously by making a multiple selection (hold down the Control key). Center the text in row 7 only.

Now we refer to the Checkbook Formulas worksheet to enter formulas. Although this looks like a lot of typing, most of the cells can be filled using a formula from an adjacent cell, so only seven entries need be made.

- Begin with G2 and G3, and enter the formulas as illustrated; then go to B10 and enter the formula given below:

Cell	Formula
G2	=G56
G3	=H56
B10	=B9+1

- Now select cells B10:B55. From the Edit menu, select Fill Down. The rest of the formulas are filled in down the column.
- Cells G9 and G10 must be typed in, as must H9 and H10. Then G10:H56 can be selected and filled down.

Cell	Formula
G9	=G5+F9−E9
G10	=G9+F10−E10
H9	=G5+(D9*F9)−(D9*E9)
H10	=H9+(D10*F10)−(D10*E10)

Figure 4-2. Top Portion of Checkbook Worksheet Showing Formulas

	A	B	C	D	E	F	G	H
1								
2					Running Balance:		=G56	
3					Last Bank Balance:		=H56	
4								
5					Opening Balance:			
6								
7	Date	Ck#	Description	I/O	Amount		Deposit	Balance	Bank Bal.
8								
9							=G5+F9-E9	=G5+(D9*F9)-(D9*E9)
10		=B9+1					=G9+F10-E10	=H9+(D10*F10)-(D10*E10)
11		=B10+1					=G10+F11-E11	=H10+(D11*F11)-(D11*E11)
12		=B11+1					=G11+F12-E12	=H11+(D12*F12)-(D12*E12)
13		=B12+1					=G12+F13-E13	=H12+(D13*F13)-(D13*E13)
14		=B13+1					=G13+F14-E14	=H13+(D14*F14)-(D14*E14)
15		=B14+1					=G14+F15-E15	=H14+(D15*F15)-(D15*E15)
16		=B15+1					=G15+F16-E16	=H15+(D16*F16)-(D16*E16)
17		=B16+1					=G16+F17-E17	=H16+(D17*F17)-(D17*E17)
18		=B17+1					=G17+F18-E18	=H17+(D18*F18)-(D18*E18)
19		=B18+1					=G18+F19-E19	=H18+(D19*F19)-(D19*E19)
20		=B19+1					=G19+F20-E20	=H19+(D20*F20)-(D20*E20)
21		=B20+1					=G20+F21-E21	=H20+(D21*F21)-(D21*E21)
22		=B21+1					=G21+F22-E22	=H21+(D22*F22)-(D22*E22)
23		=B22+1					=G22+F23-E23	=H22+(D23*F23)-(D23*E23)
24		=B23+1					=G23+F24-E24	=H23+(D24*F24)-(D24*E24)
25		=B24+1					=G24+F25-E25	=H24+(D25*F25)-(D25*E25)
26		=B25+1					=G25+F26-E26	=H25+(D26*F26)-(D26*E26)
27		=B26+1					=G26+F27-E27	=H26+(D27*F27)-(D27*E27)
28		=B27+1					=G27+F28-E28	=H27+(D28*F28)-(D28*E28)

- The cells that will contain dollar amounts must be formatted. They can all be done in one fell swoop by making a multiple selection using the Control key.
- Select G2:G3, G5, E9:H55 (you can use the shift key for this one), and G56:H56.
- From the Format menu select Number. You'll probably want to choose the format at the bottom of the list, the one that shows dollars and cents.

Figure 4-3. Bottom Portion of Checkbook Worksheet Showing Formulas

	A	B	C	D	E	F	G	H
29		=B28+1					=G28+F29-E29	=H28+(D29*F29)-(D29*E29)
30		=B29+1					=G29+F30-E30	=H29+(D30*F30)-(D30*E30)
31		=B30+1					=G30+F31-E31	=H30+(D31*F31)-(D31*E31)
32		=B31+1					=G31+F32-E32	=H31+(D32*F32)-(D32*E32)
33		=B32+1					=G32+F33-E33	=H32+(D33*F33)-(D33*E33)
34		=B33+1					=G33+F34-E34	=H33+(D34*F34)-(D34*E34)
35		=B34+1					=G34+F35-E35	=H34+(D35*F35)-(D35*E35)
36		=B35+1					=G35+F36-E36	=H35+(D36*F36)-(D36*E36)
37		=B36+1					=G36+F37-E37	=H36+(D37*F37)-(D37*E37)
38		=B37+1					=G37+F38-E38	=H37+(D38*F38)-(D38*E38)
39		=B38+1					=G38+F39-E39	=H38+(D39*F39)-(D39*E39)
40		=B39+1					=G39+F40-E40	=H39+(D40*F40)-(D40*E40)
41		=B40+1					=G40+F41-E41	=H40+(D41*F41)-(D41*E41)
42		=B41+1					=G41+F42-E42	=H41+(D42*F42)-(D42*E42)
43		=B42+1					=G42+F43-E43	=H42+(D43*F43)-(D43*E43)
44		=B43+1					=G43+F44-E44	=H43+(D44*F44)-(D44*E44)
45		=B44+1					=G44+F45-E45	=H44+(D45*F45)-(D45*E45)
46		=B45+1					=G45+F46-E46	=H45+(D46*F46)-(D46*E46)
47		=B46+1					=G46+F47-E47	=H46+(D47*F47)-(D47*E47)
48		=B47+1					=G47+F48-E48	=H47+(D48*F48)-(D48*E48)
49		=B48+1					=G48+F49-E49	=H48+(D49*F49)-(D49*E49)
50		=B49+1					=G49+F50-E50	=H49+(D50*F50)-(D50*E50)
51		=B50+1					=G50+F51-E51	=H50+(D51*F51)-(D51*E51)
52		=B51+1					=G51+F52-E52	=H51+(D52*F52)-(D52*E52)
53		=B52+1					=G52+F53-E53	=H52+(D53*F53)-(D53*E53)
54		=B53+1					=G53+F54-E54	=H53+(D54*F54)-(D54*E54)
55		=B54+1					=G54+F55-E55	=H54+(D55*F55)-(D55*E55)
56		CURRENT I					=G55+F56-E56	=H55+(D56*F56)-(D56*E56)

Two finishing touches involve names. These must be entered exactly as given for the checkbook in order for them to interact properly with the macro.

• Select D8:D55. Note that we are purposely beginning the selection with a cell outside the grid.

• From the Formula menu choose Define Name. Type in the name *OUTSTAND*.

• Now, from the File menu, select Save As and enter the name *BLANK_CB*.

Figure 4-4. Checkbook Macro

	A
1	**NEWMONTH**
2	=OPEN("BLANK_CB.XLS")
3	=ECHO(FALSE)
4	=ACTIVATE("CURNT_CB.XLS")
5	=SELECT("R3C7")
6	=COPY()
7	=ACTIVATE("BLANK_CB.XLS")
8	=SELECT("R5C7")
9	=PASTE.SPECIAL(3,1,FALSE,FALSE)
10	=SELECT("R8C1")
11	=ACTIVATE("CURNT_CB.XLS")
12	=FORMULA.GOTO("OUTSTAND")
13	=FORMULA.FIND("0",2,1,1,1)
14	=IF(A13=FALSE,GOTO(A24))
15	=SELECT("RC[-3]:RC[2]")
16	=COPY()
17	=ACTIVATE("BLANK_CB.XLS")
18	=SELECT("R[1]C")
19	=PASTE.SPECIAL(3,1,FALSE,FALSE)
20	=ACTIVATE("CURNT_CB.XLS")
21	=SELECT("RC[3]")
22	=FORMULA("")
23	=GOTO(A12)
24	=ACTIVATE("CURNT_CB.XLS")
25	=SAVE.AS?("MNTH_YR.XLS",1,"",FALSE)
26	=CLOSE()
27	=ECHO(TRUE)
28	=ACTIVATE("BLANK_CB.XLS")
29	=SAVE.AS("CURNT_CB.XLS",1,"",FALSE)
30	=RETURN()

Constructing the checkbook macro. Open a new worksheet, specifying that it be a macro sheet.
- In cell A1 enter the text *NEWMONTH*.
- From the Formula menu choose Define Name. NEWMONTH should appear in the name box.
- Check off Command in the Macro box and click OK. You might want to format cell A1 as boldface for ease of readability.

• Now type in the remaining lines exactly as listed in the illustration. When you have finished, save the macro (as CHEKMCRO).

Using the checkbook. Now you will see how easy a checkbook program is to use.

• Begin by entering your opening balance in G5.
• Now, beginning with A9, enter your check or deposit information in the normal manner.

If you have a number of entries, a convenient way to enter the information is to select the block of cells you will be using (you need only enter in columns A–F). Then, when you press Enter, the next active cell will automatically be the one you want. Notice that when you enter a check number, the next ones are filled in in sequence. If you need to alter the sequence, simply enter the appropriate number. The sequence will start again from the number you enter.

The column marked 1/0 is to indicate whether the entry is outstanding or not. More than likely, when a check is first entered it will be outstanding, so a 0 is entered in column D to indicate that. The entry will be figured in the running balance, but not in the bank balance. Replace the 0 with a 1 when the entry appears on your bank statement and is no longer outstanding. The entry will then be incorporated into the Bank Balance column.

When you have finished entering, save this file as CURNT_CB.XLS. It must be saved with this name in order to work properly with the macro. You should still have your original BLANK_CB.XLS file in the same subdirectory, and your macro sheet called CHEKMCRO.XLM.

When you are ready to close out the period and begin a new Checkbook worksheet:
• Open CURNT_CB along with CHEKMCRO.
• Reconcile the checkbook with your bank statement by entering a 1 in column D next to every confirmed entry and leaving a 0 where an entry is still outstanding. Be sure to enter any bank service charges or interest. Your Last Bank Balance should agree with your bank statement.

- To close out this worksheet and begin a new one, choose Run from the Macro menu.
- Select CHEKMCRO!NEWMONTH and click OK. The screen will oscillate while the macro closes out CURNT_CB and fills in BLANK_CB.
- Eventually you will receive the message NO MATCH, which means that the macro can't find any more outstanding entries to transfer to the new worksheet. Click OK.
- Next, you will be asked for a name under which to file the old worksheet. You might want to pick a period name such as December or ThirdQuarter.

The old worksheet is filed to disk, and the new worksheet is named CURNT_CB. You'll be asked if you want to replace the existing CURNT_CB. Click OK. Your Opening Balance will be the previous worksheet's Last Bank Balance, and the outstanding entries will be transferred.

Ledger

Purpose. This worksheet builds on the checkbook in the previous section. A number code is added to each entry which corresponds to an account number. Discrete accounts can be recorded and tracked for various categories such as rent, supplies, salaries, and so on. These accounts are displayed to the right of the checkbook.

Each account has its own individual opening balance which is carried over from the previous ledger, and a total which is passed on to the next ledger. After the accounts are named and numbered, the user need only enter the appropriate code number with each entry—the spreadsheet duplicates the entry in its correct account and adds it to the totals.

A macro closes out the current ledger and opens a new one, passing on outstanding items and previous closing balances.

Constructing the model. Follow the instructions in the previous section for setting up the BLANK_CB model. The macro in that section needn't be duplicated just yet.

Figure 4-5. Ledger Top

	A	B	C	D	E	F	G	H	I
1									
2					Running Balance:			$841.37	
3					Last Bank Balance:			$1,291.39	
4									
5					Opening Balance:			$1,202.49	
6									
7	Date	Ck#	Description	1/0	Amount	Deposit	CD	Balance	Bank Bal.
8									
9	11/1/87	304	So. Ca. Gas Co.	1	$118.90		2	$1,083.59	$1,083.59
10	11/1/87	305	Arsen Rubbish	1	$64.00		6	$1,019.59	$1,019.59
11	11/1/87	306	So. Ca. Edison	1	$60.93		3	$958.66	$958.66
12	11/1/87	307	Libert Mutual	1	$165.58		1	$793.08	$793.08
13	11/1/87	308	Apolinar Hernandez	1	$35.00		5	$758.08	$758.08
14	11/1/87		Deposit (Nugent for 11/8	1		$630.00	8	$1,388.08	$1,388.08
15	11/24/87		Interest	1		$6.09		$1,394.17	$1,394.17
16	12/1/87	309	DWP (2 mos)	1	$122.89		4	$1,271.28	$1,271.28
17	12/1/87	310	So. Ca. Gas	1	$94.23		2	$1,177.05	$1,177.05
18	12/1/87	311	So. Ca. Edison	1	$76.54		3	$1,100.51	$1,100.51
19	12/1/87	312	Liberty Mutual Ins.	1	$165.58		1	$934.93	$934.93
20	12/1/87	313	Apolinar Hernandez	1	$35.00		5	$899.93	$899.93
21	12/1/87	314	Arsen Rubbish	1	$64.00		6	$835.93	$835.93
22	12/1/87		Deposit (Nugent prepaid)	1		$450.00	8	$1,285.93	$1,285.93
23	12/22/87		Interest	1		$5.46		$1,291.39	$1,291.39
24	12/25/87	315	Hernandez (Xmas)	0	$10.00		5	$1,281.39	$1,291.39
25	1/1/88	316	Hernandez	0	$35.00		5	$1,246.39	$1,291.39
26	1/1/88	317	Liberty Mutual	0	$165.59		1	$1,080.80	$1,291.39
27	1/1/87	318	So. Ca. Gas	0	$97.25		2	$983.55	$1,291.39
28	1/1/87	319	Arsens Rubbish	0	$64.00		6	$919.55	$1,291.39

Now we will alter the checkbook model:
- Set the width of column C to 19.
- Select column G and insert a column.
- Set the width for this new column G to 2, and format the number display as General.

Figure 4-6. Ledger Bottom

	A	B	C	D	E	F	G	H	I
29	1/1/87	320	So. Ca. Edison	0	$78.18		3	$841.37	$1,291.39
30		321						$841.37	$1,291.39
31		322						$841.37	$1,291.39
32		323						$841.37	$1,291.39
33		324						$841.37	$1,291.39
34		325						$841.37	$1,291.39
35		326						$841.37	$1,291.39
36		327						$841.37	$1,291.39
37		328						$841.37	$1,291.39
38		329						$841.37	$1,291.39
39		330						$841.37	$1,291.39
40		331						$841.37	$1,291.39
41		332						$841.37	$1,291.39
42		333						$841.37	$1,291.39
43		334						$841.37	$1,291.39
44		335						$841.37	$1,291.39
45		336						$841.37	$1,291.39
46		337						$841.37	$1,291.39
47		338						$841.37	$1,291.39
48		339						$841.37	$1,291.39
49		340						$841.37	$1,291.39
50		341						$841.37	$1,291.39
51		342						$841.37	$1,291.39
52		343						$841.37	$1,291.39
53		344						$841.37	$1,291.39
54		345						$841.37	$1,291.39
55		346						$841.37	$1,291.39
56			CURRENT BALANCES					$841.37	$1,291.39

- Label this column *CD* for *code,* centering and boldfacing the label in cell G7.
- Select cells K6:S7. Place a border around the cells, checking off Outline and Left. Format these cells as boldfaced and center align them.

Figure 4-7. Ledger, Columns J–S, Rows 1–28

	J	K	L	M	N	O	P	Q	R	S
1										
2										
3										
4	Totals:	$496.75	$310.38	$215.65	$122.89	$115.00	$192.00	$0.00	$0.00	$0.00
5										
6		Insur.	Gas	Elec	DWP	Gardner	Rubbish	Misc.	Dues	Spcl. As.
7		1	2	3	4	5	6	7	8	9
8	Opening:									
9			$118.90							
10							$64.00			
11				$60.93						
12		$165.58								
13						$35.00				
14									$0.00	
15										
16					$122.89					
17			$94.23							
18				$76.54						
19		$165.58								
20						$35.00				
21							$64.00			
22									$0.00	
23										
24						$10.00				
25						$35.00				
26		$165.59								
27			$37.25							
28							$64.00			

- Type the numbers 1–9 in cells K7–S7. You might want to enter your own or the sample account names in cells K6:S6. Feel free to add more accounts, but don't forget to alter all references to these cell numbers with your new parameters.
- In cell J8 type OPENING: and align it to the right. In cell J4 type TOTALS: and align it to the right.

Figure 4-8. Ledger, Columns J–S, Rows 29–56

	J	K	L	M	N	O	P	Q	R	S
29				$78.18						
30										
31										
32										
33										
34										
35										
36										
37										
38										
39										
40										
41										
42										
43										
44										
45										
46										
47										
48										
49										
50										
51										
52										
53										
54										
55										
56		$496.75	$310.38	$215.65	$122.89	$115.00	$192.00	$0.00	$0.00	$0.00

- Select cells K8:S8 and K4:S4 and K56:S56 and add borders, checking off Outline and Left. Select cells K8:S56 and K4:S4 and format them as dollars and cents.

  Now we will enter the three ledger formulas, and fill in the rest.

- Select cell K4 and enter the illustrated formula:

  K4   =K56

Figure 4-9. Ledger Section Columns J-O, Rows 1-28

	J	K	L	M	N	O
1						
2						
3						
4	Totals:	=K56	=L56	=M56	=N56	=O56
5						
6		Insur.	Gas	Elec	DWP	Gardner
7		1	2	3	4	5
8	Opening:					
9		=IF($G9=K$7,$E9,"")	=IF($G9=L$7,$E9,"")	=IF($G9=M$7,$E9,"")	=IF($G9=N$7,$E9,"")	=IF($G9=O$7,$E9,"")
10		=IF($G10=K$7,$E10,"")	=IF($G10=L$7,$E10,"")	=IF($G10=M$7,$E10,"")	=IF($G10=N$7,$E10,"")	=IF($G10=O$7,$E10,"")
11		=IF($G11=K$7,$E11,"")	=IF($G11=L$7,$E11,"")	=IF($G11=M$7,$E11,"")	=IF($G11=N$7,$E11,"")	=IF($G11=O$7,$E11,"")
12		=IF($G12=K$7,$E12,"")	=IF($G12=L$7,$E12,"")	=IF($G12=M$7,$E12,"")	=IF($G12=N$7,$E12,"")	=IF($G12=O$7,$E12,"")
13		=IF($G13=K$7,$E13,"")	=IF($G13=L$7,$E13,"")	=IF($G13=M$7,$E13,"")	=IF($G13=N$7,$E13,"")	=IF($G13=O$7,$E13,"")
14		=IF($G14=K$7,$E14,"")	=IF($G14=L$7,$E14,"")	=IF($G14=M$7,$E14,"")	=IF($G14=N$7,$E14,"")	=IF($G14=O$7,$E14,"")
15		=IF($G15=K$7,$E15,"")	=IF($G15=L$7,$E15,"")	=IF($G15=M$7,$E15,"")	=IF($G15=N$7,$E15,"")	=IF($G15=O$7,$E15,"")
16		=IF($G16=K$7,$E16,"")	=IF($G16=L$7,$E16,"")	=IF($G16=M$7,$E16,"")	=IF($G16=N$7,$E16,"")	=IF($G16=O$7,$E16,"")
17		=IF($G17=K$7,$E17,"")	=IF($G17=L$7,$E17,"")	=IF($G17=M$7,$E17,"")	=IF($G17=N$7,$E17,"")	=IF($G17=O$7,$E17,"")
18		=IF($G18=K$7,$E18,"")	=IF($G18=L$7,$E18,"")	=IF($G18=M$7,$E18,"")	=IF($G18=N$7,$E18,"")	=IF($G18=O$7,$E18,"")
19		=IF($G19=K$7,$E19,"")	=IF($G19=L$7,$E19,"")	=IF($G19=M$7,$E19,"")	=IF($G19=N$7,$E19,"")	=IF($G19=O$7,$E19,"")
20		=IF($G20=K$7,$E20,"")	=IF($G20=L$7,$E20,"")	=IF($G20=M$7,$E20,"")	=IF($G20=N$7,$E20,"")	=IF($G20=O$7,$E20,"")
21		=IF($G21=K$7,$E21,"")	=IF($G21=L$7,$E21,"")	=IF($G21=M$7,$E21,"")	=IF($G21=N$7,$E21,"")	=IF($G21=O$7,$E21,"")
22		=IF($G22=K$7,$E22,"")	=IF($G22=L$7,$E22,"")	=IF($G22=M$7,$E22,"")	=IF($G22=N$7,$E22,"")	=IF($G22=O$7,$E22,"")
23		=IF($G23=K$7,$E23,"")	=IF($G23=L$7,$E23,"")	=IF($G23=M$7,$E23,"")	=IF($G23=N$7,$E23,"")	=IF($G23=O$7,$E23,"")
24		=IF($G24=K$7,$E24,"")	=IF($G24=L$7,$E24,"")	=IF($G24=M$7,$E24,"")	=IF($G24=N$7,$E24,"")	=IF($G24=O$7,$E24,"")
25		=IF($G25=K$7,$E25,"")	=IF($G25=L$7,$E25,"")	=IF($G25=M$7,$E25,"")	=IF($G25=N$7,$E25,"")	=IF($G25=O$7,$E25,"")
26		=IF($G26=K$7,$E26,"")	=IF($G26=L$7,$E26,"")	=IF($G26=M$7,$E26,"")	=IF($G26=N$7,$E26,"")	=IF($G26=O$7,$E26,"")
27		=IF($G27=K$7,$E27,"")	=IF($G27=L$7,$E27,"")	=IF($G27=M$7,$E27,"")	=IF($G27=N$7,$E27,"")	=IF($G27=O$7,$E27,"")
28		=IF($G28=K$7,$E28,"")	=IF($G28=L$7,$E28,"")	=IF($G28=M$7,$E28,"")	=IF($G28=N$7,$E28,"")	=IF($G28=O$7,$E28,"")

- Select cells K4:S4 and choose Fill Right from the Edit menu.
- Select cell K9 and enter the illustrated formula:

K9 =IF($G9=K$7,$E9," ")

Be sure to enter it correctly—in particular, make sure that the dollar signs are in their correct positions.

- Select K9:S55 and from the Edit menu select Fill Right. This will take a few moments. When it is done, select Fill Down. This will take even longer.
- When it is done, select K56 and enter the illustrated formula:

K56 =SUM(K8:K55)

Select K56:S56 and fill right.
- Save this file as BLANK_LG.

Figure 4-10. Ledger Section Columns J–O, Rows 29–56

	J	K	L	M	N	O
29		=IF($G29=K$7,$E29,"")	=IF($G29=L$7,$E29,"")	=IF($G29=M$7,$E29,"")	=IF($G29=N$7,$E29,"")	=IF($G29=O$7,$E29,"")
30		=IF($G30=K$7,$E30,"")	=IF($G30=L$7,$E30,"")	=IF($G30=M$7,$E30,"")	=IF($G30=N$7,$E30,"")	=IF($G30=O$7,$E30,"")
31		=IF($G31=K$7,$E31,"")	=IF($G31=L$7,$E31,"")	=IF($G31=M$7,$E31,"")	=IF($G31=N$7,$E31,"")	=IF($G31=O$7,$E31,"")
32		=IF($G32=K$7,$E32,"")	=IF($G32=L$7,$E32,"")	=IF($G32=M$7,$E32,"")	=IF($G32=N$7,$E32,"")	=IF($G32=O$7,$E32,"")
33		=IF($G33=K$7,$E33,"")	=IF($G33=L$7,$E33,"")	=IF($G33=M$7,$E33,"")	=IF($G33=N$7,$E33,"")	=IF($G33=O$7,$E33,"")
34		=IF($G34=K$7,$E34,"")	=IF($G34=L$7,$E34,"")	=IF($G34=M$7,$E34,"")	=IF($G34=N$7,$E34,"")	=IF($G34=O$7,$E34,"")
35		=IF($G35=K$7,$E35,"")	=IF($G35=L$7,$E35,"")	=IF($G35=M$7,$E35,"")	=IF($G35=N$7,$E35,"")	=IF($G35=O$7,$E35,"")
36		=IF($G36=K$7,$E36,"")	=IF($G36=L$7,$E36,"")	=IF($G36=M$7,$E36,"")	=IF($G36=N$7,$E36,"")	=IF($G36=O$7,$E36,"")
37		=IF($G37=K$7,$E37,"")	=IF($G37=L$7,$E37,"")	=IF($G37=M$7,$E37,"")	=IF($G37=N$7,$E37,"")	=IF($G37=O$7,$E37,"")
38		=IF($G38=K$7,$E38,"")	=IF($G38=L$7,$E38,"")	=IF($G38=M$7,$E38,"")	=IF($G38=N$7,$E38,"")	=IF($G38=O$7,$E38,"")
39		=IF($G39=K$7,$E39,"")	=IF($G39=L$7,$E39,"")	=IF($G39=M$7,$E39,"")	=IF($G39=N$7,$E39,"")	=IF($G39=O$7,$E39,"")
40		=IF($G40=K$7,$E40,"")	=IF($G40=L$7,$E40,"")	=IF($G40=M$7,$E40,"")	=IF($G40=N$7,$E40,"")	=IF($G40=O$7,$E40,"")
41		=IF($G41=K$7,$E41,"")	=IF($G41=L$7,$E41,"")	=IF($G41=M$7,$E41,"")	=IF($G41=N$7,$E41,"")	=IF($G41=O$7,$E41,"")
42		=IF($G42=K$7,$E42,"")	=IF($G42=L$7,$E42,"")	=IF($G42=M$7,$E42,"")	=IF($G42=N$7,$E42,"")	=IF($G42=O$7,$E42,"")
43		=IF($G43=K$7,$E43,"")	=IF($G43=L$7,$E43,"")	=IF($G43=M$7,$E43,"")	=IF($G43=N$7,$E43,"")	=IF($G43=O$7,$E43,"")
44		=IF($G44=K$7,$E44,"")	=IF($G44=L$7,$E44,"")	=IF($G44=M$7,$E44,"")	=IF($G44=N$7,$E44,"")	=IF($G44=O$7,$E44,"")
45		=IF($G45=K$7,$E45,"")	=IF($G45=L$7,$E45,"")	=IF($G45=M$7,$E45,"")	=IF($G45=N$7,$E45,"")	=IF($G45=O$7,$E45,"")
46		=IF($G46=K$7,$E46,"")	=IF($G46=L$7,$E46,"")	=IF($G46=M$7,$E46,"")	=IF($G46=N$7,$E46,"")	=IF($G46=O$7,$E46,"")
47		=IF($G47=K$7,$E47,"")	=IF($G47=L$7,$E47,"")	=IF($G47=M$7,$E47,"")	=IF($G47=N$7,$E47,"")	=IF($G47=O$7,$E47,"")
48		=IF($G48=K$7,$E48,"")	=IF($G48=L$7,$E48,"")	=IF($G48=M$7,$E48,"")	=IF($G48=N$7,$E48,"")	=IF($G48=O$7,$E48,"")
49		=IF($G49=K$7,$E49,"")	=IF($G49=L$7,$E49,"")	=IF($G49=M$7,$E49,"")	=IF($G49=N$7,$E49,"")	=IF($G49=O$7,$E49,"")
50		=IF($G50=K$7,$E50,"")	=IF($G50=L$7,$E50,"")	=IF($G50=M$7,$E50,"")	=IF($G50=N$7,$E50,"")	=IF($G50=O$7,$E50,"")
51		=IF($G51=K$7,$E51,"")	=IF($G51=L$7,$E51,"")	=IF($G51=M$7,$E51,"")	=IF($G51=N$7,$E51,"")	=IF($G51=O$7,$E51,"")
52		=IF($G52=K$7,$E52,"")	=IF($G52=L$7,$E52,"")	=IF($G52=M$7,$E52,"")	=IF($G52=N$7,$E52,"")	=IF($G52=O$7,$E52,"")
53		=IF($G53=K$7,$E53,"")	=IF($G53=L$7,$E53,"")	=IF($G53=M$7,$E53,"")	=IF($G53=N$7,$E53,"")	=IF($G53=O$7,$E53,"")
54		=IF($G54=K$7,$E54,"")	=IF($G54=L$7,$E54,"")	=IF($G54=M$7,$E54,"")	=IF($G54=N$7,$E54,"")	=IF($G54=O$7,$E54,"")
55		=IF($G55=K$7,$E55,"")	=IF($G55=L$7,$E55,"")	=IF($G55=M$7,$E55,"")	=IF($G55=N$7,$E55,"")	=IF($G55=O$7,$E55,"")
56		=SUM(K8:K55)	=SUM(L8:L55)	=SUM(M8:M55)	=SUM(N8:N55)	=SUM(O8:O55)

Figure 4-11. Ledger Section Columns P-S, Rows 1-28

	P	Q	R	S
1				
2				
3				
4	=P56	=Q56	=R56	=S56
5				
6	Rubbish	Misc.	Dues	Spcl. As.
7	6	7	8	9
8				
9	=IF($G9=P$7,$E9,"")	=IF($G9=Q$7,$E9,"")	=IF($G9=R$7,$E9,"")	=IF($G9=S$7,$E9,"")
10	=IF($G10=P$7,$E10,"")	=IF($G10=Q$7,$E10,"")	=IF($G10=R$7,$E10,"")	=IF($G10=S$7,$E10,"")
11	=IF($G11=P$7,$E11,"")	=IF($G11=Q$7,$E11,"")	=IF($G11=R$7,$E11,"")	=IF($G11=S$7,$E11,"")
12	=IF($G12=P$7,$E12,"")	=IF($G12=Q$7,$E12,"")	=IF($G12=R$7,$E12,"")	=IF($G12=S$7,$E12,"")
13	=IF($G13=P$7,$E13,"")	=IF($G13=Q$7,$E13,"")	=IF($G13=R$7,$E13,"")	=IF($G13=S$7,$E13,"")
14	=IF($G14=P$7,$E14,"")	=IF($G14=Q$7,$E14,"")	=IF($G14=R$7,$E14,"")	=IF($G14=S$7,$E14,"")
15	=IF($G15=P$7,$E15,"")	=IF($G15=Q$7,$E15,"")	=IF($G15=R$7,$E15,"")	=IF($G15=S$7,$E15,"")
16	=IF($G16=P$7,$E16,"")	=IF($G16=Q$7,$E16,"")	=IF($G16=R$7,$E16,"")	=IF($G16=S$7,$E16,"")
17	=IF($G17=P$7,$E17,"")	=IF($G17=Q$7,$E17,"")	=IF($G17=R$7,$E17,"")	=IF($G17=S$7,$E17,"")
18	=IF($G18=P$7,$E18,"")	=IF($G18=Q$7,$E18,"")	=IF($G18=R$7,$E18,"")	=IF($G18=S$7,$E18,"")
19	=IF($G19=P$7,$E19,"")	=IF($G19=Q$7,$E19,"")	=IF($G19=R$7,$E19,"")	=IF($G19=S$7,$E19,"")
20	=IF($G20=P$7,$E20,"")	=IF($G20=Q$7,$E20,"")	=IF($G20=R$7,$E20,"")	=IF($G20=S$7,$E20,"")
21	=IF($G21=P$7,$E21,"")	=IF($G21=Q$7,$E21,"")	=IF($G21=R$7,$E21,"")	=IF($G21=S$7,$E21,"")
22	=IF($G22=P$7,$E22,"")	=IF($G22=Q$7,$E22,"")	=IF($G22=R$7,$E22,"")	=IF($G22=S$7,$E22,"")
23	=IF($G23=P$7,$E23,"")	=IF($G23=Q$7,$E23,"")	=IF($G23=R$7,$E23,"")	=IF($G23=S$7,$E23,"")
24	=IF($G24=P$7,$E24,"")	=IF($G24=Q$7,$E24,"")	=IF($G24=R$7,$E24,"")	=IF($G24=S$7,$E24,"")
25	=IF($G25=P$7,$E25,"")	=IF($G25=Q$7,$E25,"")	=IF($G25=R$7,$E25,"")	=IF($G25=S$7,$E25,"")
26	=IF($G26=P$7,$E26,"")	=IF($G26=Q$7,$E26,"")	=IF($G26=R$7,$E26,"")	=IF($G26=S$7,$E26,"")
27	=IF($G27=P$7,$E27,"")	=IF($G27=Q$7,$E27,"")	=IF($G27=R$7,$E27,"")	=IF($G27=S$7,$E27,"")
28	=IF($G28=P$7,$E28,"")	=IF($G28=Q$7,$E28,"")	=IF($G28=R$7,$E28,"")	=IF($G28=S$7,$E28,"")

Figure 4-12. Ledger Section Columns P–S, Rows 29–56

	P	Q	R	S
29	=IF($G29=P$7,$E29,"")	=IF($G29=Q$7,$E29,"")	=IF($G29=R$7,$E29,"")	=IF($G29=S$7,$E29,"")
30	=IF($G30=P$7,$E30,"")	=IF($G30=Q$7,$E30,"")	=IF($G30=R$7,$E30,"")	=IF($G30=S$7,$E30,"")
31	=IF($G31=P$7,$E31,"")	=IF($G31=Q$7,$E31,"")	=IF($G31=R$7,$E31,"")	=IF($G31=S$7,$E31,"")
32	=IF($G32=P$7,$E32,"")	=IF($G32=Q$7,$E32,"")	=IF($G32=R$7,$E32,"")	=IF($G32=S$7,$E32,"")
33	=IF($G33=P$7,$E33,"")	=IF($G33=Q$7,$E33,"")	=IF($G33=R$7,$E33,"")	=IF($G33=S$7,$E33,"")
34	=IF($G34=P$7,$E34,"")	=IF($G34=Q$7,$E34,"")	=IF($G34=R$7,$E34,"")	=IF($G34=S$7,$E34,"")
35	=IF($G35=P$7,$E35,"")	=IF($G35=Q$7,$E35,"")	=IF($G35=R$7,$E35,"")	=IF($G35=S$7,$E35,"")
36	=IF($G36=P$7,$E36,"")	=IF($G36=Q$7,$E36,"")	=IF($G36=R$7,$E36,"")	=IF($G36=S$7,$E36,"")
37	=IF($G37=P$7,$E37,"")	=IF($G37=Q$7,$E37,"")	=IF($G37=R$7,$E37,"")	=IF($G37=S$7,$E37,"")
38	=IF($G38=P$7,$E38,"")	=IF($G38=Q$7,$E38,"")	=IF($G38=R$7,$E38,"")	=IF($G38=S$7,$E38,"")
39	=IF($G39=P$7,$E39,"")	=IF($G39=Q$7,$E39,"")	=IF($G39=R$7,$E39,"")	=IF($G39=S$7,$E39,"")
40	=IF($G40=P$7,$E40,"")	=IF($G40=Q$7,$E40,"")	=IF($G40=R$7,$E40,"")	=IF($G40=S$7,$E40,"")
41	=IF($G41=P$7,$E41,"")	=IF($G41=Q$7,$E41,"")	=IF($G41=R$7,$E41,"")	=IF($G41=S$7,$E41,"")
42	=IF($G42=P$7,$E42,"")	=IF($G42=Q$7,$E42,"")	=IF($G42=R$7,$E42,"")	=IF($G42=S$7,$E42,"")
43	=IF($G43=P$7,$E43,"")	=IF($G43=Q$7,$E43,"")	=IF($G43=R$7,$E43,"")	=IF($G43=S$7,$E43,"")
44	=IF($G44=P$7,$E44,"")	=IF($G44=Q$7,$E44,"")	=IF($G44=R$7,$E44,"")	=IF($G44=S$7,$E44,"")
45	=IF($G45=P$7,$E45,"")	=IF($G45=Q$7,$E45,"")	=IF($G45=R$7,$E45,"")	=IF($G45=S$7,$E45,"")
46	=IF($G46=P$7,$E46,"")	=IF($G46=Q$7,$E46,"")	=IF($G46=R$7,$E46,"")	=IF($G46=S$7,$E46,"")
47	=IF($G47=P$7,$E47,"")	=IF($G47=Q$7,$E47,"")	=IF($G47=R$7,$E47,"")	=IF($G47=S$7,$E47,"")
48	=IF($G48=P$7,$E48,"")	=IF($G48=Q$7,$E48,"")	=IF($G48=R$7,$E48,"")	=IF($G48=S$7,$E48,"")
49	=IF($G49=P$7,$E49,"")	=IF($G49=Q$7,$E49,"")	=IF($G49=R$7,$E49,"")	=IF($G49=S$7,$E49,"")
50	=IF($G50=P$7,$E50,"")	=IF($G50=Q$7,$E50,"")	=IF($G50=R$7,$E50,"")	=IF($G50=S$7,$E50,"")
51	=IF($G51=P$7,$E51,"")	=IF($G51=Q$7,$E51,"")	=IF($G51=R$7,$E51,"")	=IF($G51=S$7,$E51,"")
52	=IF($G52=P$7,$E52,"")	=IF($G52=Q$7,$E52,"")	=IF($G52=R$7,$E52,"")	=IF($G52=S$7,$E52,"")
53	=IF($G53=P$7,$E53,"")	=IF($G53=Q$7,$E53,"")	=IF($G53=R$7,$E53,"")	=IF($G53=S$7,$E53,"")
54	=IF($G54=P$7,$E54,"")	=IF($G54=Q$7,$E54,"")	=IF($G54=R$7,$E54,"")	=IF($G54=S$7,$E54,"")
55	=IF($G55=P$7,$E55,"")	=IF($G55=Q$7,$E55,"")	=IF($G55=R$7,$E55,"")	=IF($G55=S$7,$E55,"")
56	=SUM(P8:P55)	=SUM(Q8:Q55)	=SUM(R8:R55)	=SUM(S8:S55)

Constructing the macro. If you have already typed in the checkbook macro in the previous section, you have a head start in creating the ledger macro.

Simply create a new copy of CHEKMCRO and edit it according to Figure 4-13. If you haven't typed in the checkbook macro, open a new file specified as a macro sheet and type in

Figure 4-13. Ledger Macro

	A
1	NEWMONTH
2	=OPEN("BLANK_LG.XLS")
3	=ECHO(FALSE)
4	=ACTIVATE("CURNT_LG.XLS")
5	=SELECT("R3C8")
6	=COPY()
7	=ACTIVATE("BLANK_LG.XLS")
8	=SELECT("R5C8")
9	=PASTE.SPECIAL(3,1,FALSE,FALSE)
10	=ACTIVATE("CURNT_LG.XLS")
11	=SELECT("R56C11:R56C19")
12	=COPY()
13	=ACTIVATE("BLANK_LG.XLS")
14	=SELECT("R8C11:R8C19")
15	=PASTE.SPECIAL(3,1,FALSE,FALSE)
16	=SELECT("R8C1")
17	=ACTIVATE("CURNT_LG.XLS")
18	=FORMULA.GOTO("OUTSTAND")
19	=FORMULA.FIND("0",2,1,1)
20	=IF(A19=FALSE,GOTO(A33))
21	=SELECT("RC[-3]:RC[3]")
22	=COPY()
23	=ACTIVATE("BLANK_LG.XLS")
24	=SELECT("R[1]C")
25	=PASTE.SPECIAL(3,1,FALSE,FALSE)
26	=SELECT("RC[6]")
27	=FORMULA("="""*""")
28	=SELECT("RC[-6]")
29	=ACTIVATE("CURNT_LG.XLS")
30	=SELECT("RC[3]")
31	=FORMULA("")
32	=GOTO(A16)
33	=SAVE.AS?("MNTH_YR.XLS",1)
34	=CLOSE()
35	=ECHO(TRUE)
36	=ACTIVATE("BLANK_LG.XLS")
37	=SELECT("R9C4:R55C4")
38	=DEFINE.NAME("OUTSTAND","=R8C4:R55C4")
39	=SAVE.AS("CURNT_LG",1)
40	=RETURN()

the macro as illustrated. Select cell A1, define the name as NEWMONTH, and check off Command before clicking OK (this has already been done if you are editing CHEKMCRO). Save this file as LDGRMCRO.

Using the ledger. Read the instructions for using the checkbook in the previous section. The ledger operates the same way, with the addition of the accounts feature.

- Open the file BLANK_LG and fill in cells K6:S6 with your account names. Make a note of which names correspond to which numbers. Also fill in cells K8:S8 with opening account balances.
- When making check entries, fill in the code column (CD) with the number of the appropriate account. You can leave this column blank if you are entering a deposit, or you do not want the entry assigned to an account.
- When you've entered a code number, the amount is automatically entered in its account column, and the account total updated.
- Upon finishing the entries, save this file as CURNT_LG.

You should still have the file BLANK_LG in the same subdirectory. When you are ready to close out the current ledger and begin a new one:

- Open the file LDGRMCRO along with CURNT_LG.
- Run NEWMONTH by selecting Run from the Macro menu.

The screen will oscillate between CURNT_LG and BLANK_LG as the macro fills in all the running totals and outstanding entries (see the checkbook section for a complete explanation).

Eventually you will see the message NO MATCH, which means that no more outstanding items can be found. Click OK. You will now be asked under what name you wish to file the old ledger. A period name is recommended, such as FEB_87 or 1ST_QRTR. The old ledger will be saved, and the new ledger will be renamed CURNT_LG and displayed. You'll notice that the outstanding entries are given an asterisk (*) in the code column, indicating that these amounts are already in the opening account balances and should not be entered into the account columns again.

Always use the name CURNT_LG for the ledger in use, and always keep the files BLANK_LG and LDGRMCRO in the same subdirectory as CURNT_LG so that the macro will operate properly.

Tracking Cashflow

Figure 4-14. Columns A–E

	A	B	C	D	E
1		January	February	March	
2	Income 1	$4,530.00	$6,670.00	$8,500.00	
3	Income 2	$7,500.00	$7,200.00	$0.00	
4	Income 3	$3,000.00	$2,560.00	$5,000.00	
5					
6	Totals	$15,030.00	$16,430.00	$13,500.00	
7					
8		30 DAYS	60 DAYS	90 DAYS	
9		20%	60%	20%	
10					
11	Cash Receipts:	$3,006.00	$12,304.00	$15,564.00	
12					
13	Receivables:	$12,024.00	$16,150.00	$14,086.00	
14					
15					
16					
17					
18					
19					
20					
21					
22					
23					
24					
25					
26					
27					
28					
29					
30					
31					
32					
33					
34					
35					
36					
37					
38					
39					
40					
41					
42					
43					
44					

Figure 4-15. Columns F–J, Rows 1–34

	F	G	H	I	J
1					
2	Date	Description	Receipts	Disbursements	Balance
3	Jan			Opening:	$2,200.00
4	*1-Jan*	*From Cashflow*	$1,503.00		$3,703.00
5					$3,703.00
6	3-Jan	Salaries		$1,805.00	$1,898.00
7					$1,898.00
8	10-Jan	Insurance		$400.00	$1,498.00
9					$1,498.00
10					$1,498.00
11	12-Jan	Supplies		$1,200.00	$298.00
12					$298.00
13					$298.00
14	*15-Jan*	*From Cashflow*	$1,503.00		$1,801.00
15					$1,801.00
16					$1,801.00
17	20-Jan	Salaries		$1,805.00	($4.00)
18					($4.00)
19					($4.00)
20	25-Jan	Utilities		$750.00	($754.00)
21					($754.00)
22					($754.00)
23					($754.00)
24	30-Jan	Rent		$2,000.00	($2,754.00)
25	Feb				($2,754.00)
26	*1-Feb*	*From Cashflow*	$6,152.00		$3,398.00
27					$3,398.00
28	3-Feb	Salaries		$1,805.00	$1,593.00
29					$1,593.00
30	10-Feb	Insurance		$400.00	$1,193.00
31					$1,193.00
32					$1,193.00
33	12-Feb	Supplies		$1,200.00	($7.00)
34					($7.00)

Figure 4-16. Columns F–J, Rows 35–68

	F	G	H	I	J
35					($7.00)
36	*15-Feb*	*From Cashflow*	$6,152.00		$6,145.00
37					$6,145.00
38	20-Feb	Salaries		$1,805.00	$4,340.00
39					$4,340.00
40					$4,340.00
41	25-Feb	Utilities		$750.00	$3,590.00
42					$3,590.00
43					$3,590.00
44					$3,590.00
45					$3,590.00
46	28-Feb	Rent		$2,000.00	$1,590.00
47	Mar				$1,590.00
48	*1-Mar*	*From Cashflow*	$7,782.00		$9,372.00
49					$9,372.00
50	3-Mar	Salaries		$1,805.00	$7,567.00
51					$7,567.00
52	10-Mar	Insurance		$400.00	$7,167.00
53					$7,167.00
54					$7,167.00
55	12-Mar	Supplies		$1,200.00	$5,967.00
56					$5,967.00
57					$5,967.00
58	*15-Mar*	*From Cashflow*	$7,782.00		$13,749.00
59					$13,749.00
60	20-Mar	Salaries		$1,805.00	$11,944.00
61					$11,944.00
62					$11,944.00
63	25-Mar	Utilities		$750.00	$11,194.00
64					$11,194.00
65					$11,194.00
66					$11,194.00
67					$11,194.00
68	30-Mar	Rent		*$2,000.00*	$9,194.00

Purpose. Projecting cashflow is one of the most difficult and important aspects of running a business. Getting caught with insufficient cash on hand can wipe out an otherwise thriving business. On the other hand, not getting the most out of excess cash can thwart the growth of a business. This model aids in projecting cashflow over a three-month period. It can be expanded to cover a longer time period.

The worksheet contains two sections. In the first section, the user enters expected total sales from three separate profit centers over three months. The expected collection time is then entered in the form of what percentage of the month's sales will be received within 30 days and what percentage will be received within 60 days. The 90-day percentage figure is automatically calculated and filled in by finding the remainder. (These percentages can be derived by use of the Accounts Receivable worksheet below.) Then cash receipts for each separate month are calculated, along with receivables as of that month.

In the second section of the worksheet, the three-month period is laid out so that known receipts and disbursements can be entered and the running balance monitored. The worksheet takes the cash receipts from the first section and incorporates them into the schedule.

In the illustrated example, the cash receipts for a month are divided in half, with the first half being entered on the first of the month and the second half entered on the fifteenth. Of course, this schedule can be altered to conform to your business.

What-if projections are done simply by plugging different percentages or sales figures into the first part of the worksheet and instantly seeing what the effect is on the running balance.

Constructing the model. To create the cashflow tracking spreadsheet:
• Open a worksheet and clear away the gridlines with the Display selection on the Options menu.

• Select column A and widen the column to 14.85. Column F should be set to 8.5, and column G to 28.28. The other columns (B, C, D, E, H, I, J) should be set at 11.

• Select cells B8:D9 and add an outlined border with the Border selection on the Format menu. Select cells F2:J2 and outline them also.

• Now select cell ranges F3:J24, F26:J46, and F48:J68 (multiple selections are done by holding down the Control key when entering the additional ranges). Format these cells with complete borders by checking off everything except Shading on the Border menu.

Now the headings can be entered as indicated in the illustration. They are to be boldfaced with the Fonts selection on the Format menu. Some are centered and some are not—use the illustration as your guide. The headings at H2:J2 seem to be in three different cells, but actually the words *Receipts Disbursements Balance* are all entered into cell H2.

In this manner, the column widths can be narrower than the labels that head them. These columns are kept narrow so that the entire cashflow timetable can be viewed on the screen. Notice that the headings *From Cashflow* are italicized. This is to differentiate them from entries, and they should appear on the blank Cashflow sheet (the one which has not been filled in).

• Now select cell J3 and ranges H4:J68, B2:D6, and B11:D13. Format these as dollars and cents with the Number selection on the Format menu. If you have a color system, you might want to choose the Red (for negative numbers) selection so that potentially weak periods stand out more readily on the worksheet.

• Select cells B9:D9 and format these as percents with the same selection as above. You will need to scroll down one screen to find the percentage formats.

Figure 4-17. Columns A–E, Rows 1–16

	A	B	C	D	E
1		January	February	March	
2	Income 1				
3	Income 2				
4	Income 3				
5					
6	Totals	=SUM(B2:B4)	=SUM(C2:C4)	=SUM(D2:D4)	
7					
8		30 DAYS	60 DAYS	90 DAYS	
9				=1-C9-B9	
10					
11	Cash Receipts:	=B9*B6	=(B9*C6)+(C9*B6)	=(B9*D6)+(C9*C6)+(D9*B6)	
12					
13	Receivables:	=B6-B11	=(B6+C6)-(B11+C11)	=(D6+C6+B6)-(B11+C11+D11)	
14					
15					
16					

Now we will enter the formulas.

• Select cell B6 and enter the formula as illustrated:

B6 =SUM(B2:B4)

• Select cells B6:D6 and choose Fill Right from the Edit menu to enter formulas into these cells. The formulas in cells D9, B11:D11, and B13:D13 must all be typed in by hand—they cannot be filled—and likewise for cells H4, H14, H26, H36, H48, and H58.

Cell	Formula
D9	=1−C9−B9
B11	=B9*B6
C11	=(B9*C6)+(C9*B6)
D11	=(B9*D6)+(C9*C6)+(D9*B6)
B13	=B6−B11
C13	=(B6+C6)−(B11+C11)
D13	=(D6+C6+B6)−(B11+C11+D11)
H4	=B11/2
H14	=B11/2
H26	=C11/2
H36	=C11/2
H48	=D11/2
H58	=D11/2

Figure 4-18. Columns F-J, Rows 1-34

	F	G	H	I	J
1					
2	Date	Description	Receipts Di:		
3	Jan			Open	
4	*32143*	*From Cashflow*	=B11/2		=J3+H4-I4
5					=J4+H5-I5
6					=J5+H6-I6
7					=J6+H7-I7
8					=J7+H8-I8
9					=J8+H9-I9
10					=J9+H10-I10
11					=J10+H11-I11
12					=J11+H12-I12
13					=J12+H13-I13
14	*32157*	*From Cashflow*	=B11/2		=J13+H14-I14
15					=J14+H15-I15
16					=J15+H16-I16
17					=J16+H17-I17
18					=J17+H18-I18
19					=J18+H19-I19
20					=J19+H20-I20
21					=J20+H21-I21
22					=J21+H22-I22
23					=J22+H23-I23
24					=J23+H24-I24
25	Feb				=J24+H25-I25
26	*32174*	*From Cashflow*	=C11/2		=J25+H26-I26
27					=J26+H27-I27
28					=J27+H28-I28
29					=J28+H29-I29
30					=J29+H30-I30
31					=J30+H31-I31
32					=J31+H32-I32
33					=J32+H33-I33
34					=J33+H34-I34

Figure 4-19. Columns F–J, Rows 35–68

	F	G	H	I	J
35					=J34+H35-I35
36	*32188*	*From Cashflow*	=C11/2		=J35+H36-I36
37					=J36+H37-I37
38					=J37+H38-I38
39					=J38+H39-I39
40					=J39+H40-I40
41					=J40+H41-I41
42					=J41+H42-I42
43					=J42+H43-I43
44					=J43+H44-I44
45					=J44+H45-I45
46					=J45+H46-I46
47	Mar				=J46+H47-I47
48	*32203*	*From Cashflow*	=D11/2		=J47+H48-I48
49					=J48+H49-I49
50					=J49+H50-I50
51					=J50+H51-I51
52					=J51+H52-I52
53					=J52+H53-I53
54					=J53+H54-I54
55					=J54+H55-I55
56					=J55+H56-I56
57					=J56+H57-I57
58	*32217*	*From Cashflow*	=D11/2		=J57+H58-I58
59					=J58+H59-I59
60					=J59+H60-I60
61					=J60+H61-I61
62					=J61+H62-I62
63					=J62+H63-I63
64					=J63+H64-I64
65					=J64+H65-I65
66					=J65+H66-I66
67					=J66+H67-I67
68					=J67+H68-I68

After you have typed in the formulas for these cells, your work is nearly finished.

- Select J4 and type in the formula as illustrated; note that the last address reads I4 and is *not* the number 14:

J4 = J3 + H4 − I4

- Select cells J4:J68, and fill down by choosing this from the Edit menu.

Using Cashflow. To use your Cashflow worksheet:

- Enter projected sales from three separate profit centers for three months in cells B2:D4.
- Enter projected cash receipt percentages into cells B9:C9.

Cell D9 is calculated by finding the remainder. What these numbers signify is that, for example, 20 percent of your receivables will arrive within 30 days, 60 percent will arrive within 60 days, and the remaining 20 percent will arrive within 90 days. When these numbers are entered, your actual cash receipts for each month are calculated and displayed in cells B11:D11, and your receivables are displayed in cells B13:D13.

Now scroll over to the timetable. Columns F–J should fit perfectly on the screen. You'll see that the figures from the first section are transferred over and entered under receipts. In the example, each month's receipts are divided in half and entered on the first and the fifteenth. This can easily be altered if necessary.

- Enter all known disbursements for the three-month period as indicated in the illustration. In column J you will see your running balance for the period.

Now you can perform what-if calculations.

- Go back to the first section of the worksheet and size the window to include only rows 1–9 and only columns A-D.
- Drag this window to the upper midsection of your screen.
- Now select the New Window option from the Window menu. Size this window to include only columns F–J and only about seven rows.
- Position this window at the bottom center of your screen.

You should be able to see all the way down to row 9 on the top window. You can now scroll the bottom window to whatever rows are pertinent, and change the entries in the top window to see what effect this has on your cashflow.

Tracking Accounts Receivable

Purpose. This model tracks the pattern of your receivables. You enter the date payment is received, the date of the original invoice, and the amount paid. The worksheet calculates how many days it took to receive payment and what percentage of your receivables arrived in 30, 60, 90, and more than 90 days. This information can be used to project cashflow (enter the percentages into the Cashflow worksheet) and to time disbursements.

Constructing the model. On a new worksheet:
• Set the column widths (with that selection on the Format menu) as follows:

Column	Width
A	8
B	10
C	8
E–I	7

You should be able to see columns A–I in their entirety on your screen. If you can't, you can enlarge the window to fill the entire screen.
• From the Options menu, select Display and clear away the gridlines by unchecking that selection.
• Select the following cells and ranges simultaneously by using the multiple selection technique (hold down the Control key while clicking additional cells): A3:I3, B4, E4:I4, B26, E26:I26.
• From the Format menu, choose Border and check off all selections except Shading.
• Type in the headings as illustrated.
• Using selections from the Format menu, boldface the headings and center-align all of them except for the following: *Sum* in A26 is right-aligned, and *Totals:* is in C26 with 10 spaces preceding it ("   Totals") in order for it to line up properly.

Figure 4-20. Accounts Receivable Model

	A	B	C	D	E	F	G	H	I
1									
2									
3	Date	Amount	Inv. Date	Days	Cash	30	60	90	90+
4		$9,214.45			12.75%	13.07%	35.54%	33.88%	4.76%
5	4/1/88	$185.00	2/21/88	40			1.53%		
6	4/3/88	$500.00	12/16/87	109					4.14%
7	4/4/88	$640.00	4/3/88	1	5.29%				
8	4/4/88	$1,280.00	2/1/88	63				10.59%	
9	4/6/88	$450.70	3/8/88	29		3.73%			
10	4/10/88	$750.80	4/10/88	0	6.21%				
11	4/14/88	$234.56	2/2/88	72				1.94%	
12	4/16/88	$2,310.90	3/2/88	45			19.12%		
13	4/16/88	$75.00	4/15/87	367					0.62%
14	4/20/88	$458.91	4/5/88	15		3.80%			
15	4/21/88	$2,580.80	1/27/88	85				21.35%	
16	4/24/88	$670.20	4/16/88	8		5.54%			
17	4/28/88	$150.70	4/28/88	0	1.25%				
18	4/30/88	$1,800.00	3/10/88	51			14.89%		
19									
20									
21									
22									
23									
24									
25									
26	Sum:	$12,087.57		Totals:	12.75%	13.07%	35.54%	33.88%	4.76%

- Select cells B4:B26 and format them as dollars and cents by choosing the bottom selection from the Number submenu, which in turn is found under the Format menu.
- Select cell ranges A5:A25 and C5:C25 and format them as dates by choosing m/d/yy, also from the Number submenu (you'll have to scroll down one screen to find this selection).

• Now select cells E4:I26 and format these as percents by choosing 0.00% (also down one screen) on the Number submenu.

Figure 4-21. Columns A–F, Rows 1–26

	A	B	C	D	E	F
1						
2						
3	Date	Amount	Inv. Date	Days	Cash	30
4		=B26			=E26	=F26
5				=IF(A5>0,A5-C5,"")	=IF(AND(D5<2,B5>0),B5/$B$26,"")	=IF(AND(D5>1,D5<31),B5/$B$26,"")
6				=IF(A6>0,A6-C6,"")	=IF(AND(D6<2,B6>0),B6/$B$26,"")	=IF(AND(D6>1,D6<31),B6/$B$26,"")
7				=IF(A7>0,A7-C7,"")	=IF(AND(D7<2,B7>0),B7/$B$26,"")	=IF(AND(D7>1,D7<31),B7/$B$26,"")
8				=IF(A8>0,A8-C8,"")	=IF(AND(D8<2,B8>0),B8/$B$26,"")	=IF(AND(D8>1,D8<31),B8/$B$26,"")
9				=IF(A9>0,A9-C9,"")	=IF(AND(D9<2,B9>0),B9/$B$26,"")	=IF(AND(D9>1,D9<31),B9/$B$26,"")
10				=IF(A10>0,A11-C10,"")	=IF(AND(D10<2,B10>0),B10/$B$26,"")	=IF(AND(D10>1,D10<31),B10/$B$26,"")
11				=IF(A11>0,A11-C11,"")	=IF(AND(D11<2,B11>0),B11/$B$26,"")	=IF(AND(D11>1,D11<31),B11/$B$26,"")
12				=IF(A12>0,A12-C12,"")	=IF(AND(D12<2,B12>0),B12/$B$26,"")	=IF(AND(D12>1,D12<31),B12/$B$26,"")
13				=IF(A13>0,A13-C13,"")	=IF(AND(D13<2,B13>0),B13/$B$26,"")	=IF(AND(D13>1,D13<31),B13/$B$26,"")
14				=IF(A14>0,A14-C14,"")	=IF(AND(D14<2,B14>0),B14/$B$26,"")	=IF(AND(D14>1,D14<31),B14/$B$26,"")
15				=IF(A15>0,A15-C15,"")	=IF(AND(D15<2,B15>0),B15/$B$26,"")	=IF(AND(D15>1,D15<31),B15/$B$26,"")
16				=IF(A16>0,A16-C16,"")	=IF(AND(D16<2,B16>0),B16/$B$26,"")	=IF(AND(D16>1,D16<31),B16/$B$26,"")
17				=IF(A17>0,A17-C17,"")	=IF(AND(D17<2,B17>0),B17/$B$26,"")	=IF(AND(D17>1,D17<31),B17/$B$26,"")
18				=IF(A18>0,A18-C18,"")	=IF(AND(D18<2,B18>0),B18/$B$26,"")	=IF(AND(D18>1,D18<31),B18/$B$26,"")
19				=IF(A19>0,A19-C19,"")	=IF(AND(D19<2,B19>0),B19/$B$26,"")	=IF(AND(D19>1,D19<31),B19/$B$26,"")
20				=IF(A20>0,A20-C20,"")	=IF(AND(D20<2,B20>0),B20/$B$26,"")	=IF(AND(D20>1,D20<31),B20/$B$26,"")
21				=IF(A21>0,A21-C21,"")	=IF(AND(D21<2,B21>0),B21/$B$26,"")	=IF(AND(D21>1,D21<31),B21/$B$26,"")
22				=IF(A22>0,A22-C22,"")	=IF(AND(D22<2,B22>0),B22/$B$26,"")	=IF(AND(D22>1,D22<31),B22/$B$26,"")
23				=IF(A23>0,A23-C23,"")	=IF(AND(D23<2,B23>0),B23/$B$26,"")	=IF(AND(D23>1,D23<31),B23/$B$26,"")
24				=IF(A24>0,A24-C24,"")	=IF(AND(D24<2,B24>0),B24/$B$26,"")	=IF(AND(D24>1,D24<31),B24/$B$26,"")
25				=IF(A25>0,A25-C25,"")	=IF(AND(D25<2,B25>0),B25/$B$26,"")	=IF(AND(D25>1,D25<31),B25/$B$26,"")
26	Sum:	=SUM(B5:B25)	To		=SUM(E5:E25)	=SUM(F5:F25)

Entering the formulas looks like a lot of typing, but through the miracle of the Fill command it is actually quite simple.

• Select B4 and enter the formula illustrated:

B4 =B26

• Select E4 and enter its illustrated formula, and then select cells E4:I4 and choose Fill Right from the Edit menu:

E4 =E26

• Now select cell D5, enter the illustrated formula, select cells D5:D25, and fill these by choosing Fill Down from the Edit menu.

Figure 4-22. Columns G-I, Rows 1-26

	G	H	I
1			
2			
3	60	90	90+
4	=G26	=H26	=I26
5	=IF(AND(D5>30,D5<61),B5/$B$26,"")	=IF(AND(D5>60,D5<91),B5/$B$26,"")	=IF(AND(D5>90,B5>0),B5/$B$26,"")
6	=IF(AND(D6>30,D6<61),B6/$B$26,"")	=IF(AND(D6>60,D6<91),B6/$B$26,"")	=IF(AND(D6>90,B6>0),B6/$B$26,"")
7	=IF(AND(D7>30,D7<61),B7/$B$26,"")	=IF(AND(D7>60,D7<91),B7/$B$26,"")	=IF(AND(D7>90,B7>0),B7/$B$26,"")
8	=IF(AND(D8>30,D8<61),B8/$B$26,"")	=IF(AND(D8>60,D8<91),B8/$B$26,"")	=IF(AND(D8>90,B8>0),B8/$B$26,"")
9	=IF(AND(D9>30,D9<61),B9/$B$26,"")	=IF(AND(D9>60,D9<91),B9/$B$26,"")	=IF(AND(D9>90,B9>0),B9/$B$26,"")
10	=IF(AND(D10>30,D10<61),B10/$B$26,"")	=IF(AND(D10>60,D10<91),B10/$B$26,"")	=IF(AND(D10>90,B10>0),B10/$B$26,"")
11	=IF(AND(D11>30,D11<61),B11/$B$26,"")	=IF(AND(D11>60,D11<91),B11/$B$26,"")	=IF(AND(D11>90,B11>0),B11/$B$26,"")
12	=IF(AND(D12>30,D12<61),B12/$B$26,"")	=IF(AND(D12>60,D12<91),B12/$B$26,"")	=IF(AND(D12>90,B12>0),B12/$B$26,"")
13	=IF(AND(D13>30,D13<61),B13/$B$26,"")	=IF(AND(D13>60,D13<91),B13/$B$26,"")	=IF(AND(D13>90,B13>0),B13/$B$26,"")
14	=IF(AND(D14>30,D14<61),B14/$B$26,"")	=IF(AND(D14>60,D14<91),B14/$B$26,"")	=IF(AND(D14>90,B14>0),B14/$B$26,"")
15	=IF(AND(D15>30,D15<61),B15/$B$26,"")	=IF(AND(D15>60,D15<91),B15/$B$26,"")	=IF(AND(D15>90,B15>0),B15/$B$26,"")
16	=IF(AND(D16>30,D16<61),B16/$B$26,"")	=IF(AND(D16>60,D16<91),B16/$B$26,"")	=IF(AND(D16>90,B16>0),B16/$B$26,"")
17	=IF(AND(D17>30,D17<61),B17/$B$26,"")	=IF(AND(D17>60,D17<91),B17/$B$26,"")	=IF(AND(D17>90,B17>0),B17/$B$26,"")
18	=IF(AND(D18>30,D18<61),B18/$B$26,"")	=IF(AND(D18>60,D18<91),B18/$B$26,"")	=IF(AND(D18>90,B18>0),B18/$B$26,"")
19	=IF(AND(D19>30,D19<61),B19/$B$26,"")	=IF(AND(D19>60,D19<91),B19/$B$26,"")	=IF(AND(D19>90,B19>0),B19/$B$26,"")
20	=IF(AND(D20>30,D20<61),B20/$B$26,"")	=IF(AND(D20>60,D20<91),B20/$B$26,"")	=IF(AND(D20>90,B20>0),B20/$B$26,"")
21	=IF(AND(D21>30,D21<61),B21/$B$26,"")	=IF(AND(D21>60,D21<91),B21/$B$26,"")	=IF(AND(D21>90,B21>0),B21/$B$26,"")
22	=IF(AND(D22>30,D22<61),B22/$B$26,"")	=IF(AND(D22>60,D22<91),B22/$B$26,"")	=IF(AND(D22>90,B22>0),B22/$B$26,"")
23	=IF(AND(D23>30,D23<61),B23/$B$26,"")	=IF(AND(D23>60,D23<91),B23/$B$26,"")	=IF(AND(D23>90,B23>0),B23/$B$26,"")
24	=IF(AND(D24>30,D24<61),B24/$B$26,"")	=IF(AND(D24>60,D24<91),B24/$B$26,"")	=IF(AND(D24>90,B24>0),B24/$B$26,"")
25	=IF(AND(D25>30,D25<61),B25/$B$26,"")	=IF(AND(D25>60,D25<91),B25/$B$26,"")	=IF(AND(D25>90,B25>0),B25/$B$26,"")
26	=SUM(G5:G25)	=SUM(H5:H25)	=SUM(I5:I25)

D5 =IF(A5>0,A5−C5,"")

- Repeat these steps by entering the formulas into E5, F5, G5, H5, and I5.

Cell   Formula

E5   =IF(AND(D5<2,B5>0),B5/$B$26," ")
F5   =IF(AND(D5>1,D5<31),B5/$B$26," ")
G5   =IF(AND(D5>30,D5<61),B5/$B$26," ")
H5   =IF(AND(D5>60,D5<91),B5/$B$26," ")
I5   =IF(AND(D5>90,B5>0),B5/$B$26," ")

- Choose cells E5:I25 and fill down.
- All that remains now is row 26. Enter the illustrated formulas into cells B26 and E26:

B26   =SUM(B5:B25)
E26   =SUM(E5:E25)

Select cells E26:I26 and fill right.

If the formulas seem overly complex for the job they are doing—particularly the formulas which contain *IF* and *AND*—these are written not only to produce the correct value, but to eliminate the display of zeros in blank cells. This method was chosen over the unchecking of Zero Values from the Display selection on the Options menu, since there are certain cells in which we want to see zero values.

Using the receivables model. This worksheet can be set up to accommodate any length of time. In the example it is used during a one-month period. As payments arrive, enter them onto the worksheet. List first the current date, then the amount received, then the date of the original invoice. The worksheet will calculate the number of days it took to collect, and this number will appear in the Days column. The percentage in the same row as the entry will appear in the appropriate column to reflect the broader collection period: Cash (within 1 day), within 30 days, within 60 days, within 90 days, and more than 90 days.

The percentage number itself reflects what percentage of the total payments received thus far this individual entry represents. In the boxes at the top and bottom of the columns are the total percentages for the column. This tells you, for example, that 12.75 percent of your sales was cash, 13.07 percent was received within 30 days, 35.54 percent was received within 60 days, 33.88 percent was received within 90 days, and 4.76 percent took more than 90 days to collect.

This data can be very useful to project cashflow and plan disbursement timing. In fact, these numbers can be plugged right into the Cashflow worksheet.

Determining Sales Productivity

Purpose. In any type of business that involves a sales force, it is useful to be able to determine the productivity of the salespeople at a glance. This model allows the user to determine quickly both total production by month as well as total production by salesperson by years. In addition, it automatically calculates the sales commission paid.

Figure 4-23. Sales Productivity Worksheet

	A	B	C	D	E	F	G	H	I
1		Fred	Wilma	Barney	Betty	Dino	Bam-Bam	Tot. sales	Commis.
2	Jan-88	$1,200.00	$965.00	$1,500.00	$1,876.00	$876.00	$65.00	$6,482.00	$648.20
3	Feb-88	$850.00	$1,020.00	$1,456.00	$2,167.00	$895.00	$74.00	$6,462.00	$646.20
4	Mar-88	$756.00	$942.00	$1,700.00	$864.00	$790.00	$0.00	$5,052.00	$505.20
5	Apr-88	$1,123.00	$850.00	$1,900.00	$935.00	$543.00	$0.00	$5,351.00	$535.10
6	May-88	$2,140.00	$1,345.00	$3,421.00	$1,045.00	$586.00	$32.00	$8,569.00	$856.90
7	Jun-88	$1,760.00	$1,442.00	$970.00	$1,067.00	$331.00	$80.00	$5,650.00	$565.00
8	Jul-88	$223.00	$1,200.00	$2,311.00	$1,348.00	$278.00	$17.80	$5,377.80	$537.78
9	Aug-88	$450.00	$1,180.00	$2,312.00	$1,609.00	$302.00	$97.90	$6,550.90	$655.09
10	Sep-88	$3,390.00	$450.00	$1,897.00	$1,354.00	$998.00	$56.00	$8,145.00	$814.50
11	Oct-88	$1,650.00	$765.00	$1,765.00	$1,278.00	$690.00	$65.00	$6,213.00	$621.30
12	Nov-88	$900.00	$1,123.00	$1,285.00	$1,286.00	$654.00	$61.96	$5,309.96	$531.00
13	Dec-88	$1,200.00	$2,001.00	$1,234.00	$1,534.00	$653.00	$21.80	$6,643.80	$664.38
14									
15	Total	$15,642.00	$13,283.00	$21,751.00	$16,363.00	$8,196.00	$571.46	$75,806.46	
16	Comm.	$1,564.20	$1,328.30	$2,175.10	$1,636.30	$819.60	$57.15		$7,580.65

Constructing the model. To create the sales productivity spreadsheet:

• Open a new worksheet. Select column widths depending on the size of names used.
• Insert the first date in cell A2 (using one of the standard *Excel* formats as indicated here); then fill downward for as many dates as needed by highlighting and using the Data, Series command.
• Fill in the names and titles that are appropriate to your application or use those shown here.
• Fill in the formulas as indicated. The sales commission formula (row 16) currently shows a 10-percent commission. This can, of course, be changed to any commission rate desired. (The formulas need not all be filled in by hand—just type the first one, then use the Fill command to fill the remaining cells.)

Figure 4-24. Starting the Worksheet

	A	B	C	D	E
1		Fred	Wilma	Barney	Betty
2					
3					
4					
5					
6					
7					
8					
9					
10					
11					
12					
13					
14					
15	Total	=SUM(B2:B13)	=SUM(C2:C13)	=SUM(D2:D13)	=SUM(E2:E13)
16	Comm.	=0.1*B15	=0.1*C15	=0.1*D15	=0.1*E15

Figure 4-25. The Worksheet, Columns F–I, Rows 1–16

	F	G	H	I
1	Dino	Bam-Bam	Tot. sales	Commis.
2			=SUM(B2:G2)	=0.1*H2
3				=0.1*H3
4				=0.1*H4
5				=0.1*H5
6				=0.1*H6
7				=0.1*H7
8				=0.1*H8
9				=0.1*H9
10				=0.1*H10
11				=0.1*H11
12				=0.1*H12
13				=0.1*H13
14				
15	=SUM(F2:F13)	=SUM(G2:G13)	=SUM(H2:H13)	
16	=0.1*F15	=0.1*G15		=SUM(I2:I13)

Using the model. Insert the sales production figures for each salesperson. The model will automatically calculate total sales and total commissions by month on the right. It will automatically calculate total sales and commissions *by salesperson* at the bottom.

Charting. This type of application lends itself to graphic description. The attached charts were developed using the previous worksheet data. (A chart is created by selecting the range of cells containing the data you wish to chart, then choosing the Chart selection from the New option on the File menu.)

Figure 4-26. Chart Example

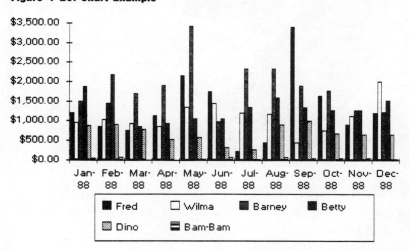

Figure 4-27. Chart Example

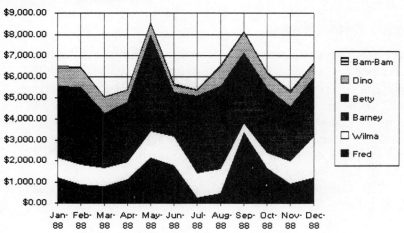

Figure 4-28. Pie Chart

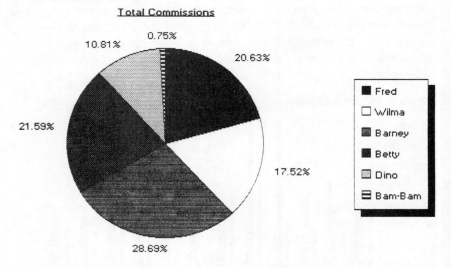

Real Estate Applications

The real estate applications created in this section are:
• Finding present value
• Determining future value
• Finding the interest rate
• Amortizing a mortgage

Finding Present Value

Purpose. Enter the annual interest rate, term of the loan, payment per period, and future value, and the worksheet will compute the present value (or outstanding principal of the loan). This can be useful if, for example, a mortgage buyer wants to know how much it would cost to pay off a mortgage early. (Obviously, this worksheet only figures outstanding principal and does not take into account penalties or extra costs of prepaying a mortgage.)

The worksheet also computes the status of the loan after a given number of payments.

Figure 4-29. Present Value Worksheet

	A	B	C	D
1	(Boldface=User Entry)			
2	Interest Rate (annual)	9.00%	Interest Rate (monthly)	0.75%
3	Term of Loan (months)	360		
4	Monthly Payment	$950.00		
5	Future Value	$106,500.00		
6				
7	Present Value	$125,297.63	total amount owed	$448,500.00
8				
9	payment #	20	number of payments remaining	340
10	total paid to date	$19,000.00	total of remaining payments	$429,500.00
11				
12	principal remaining	$125,076.97	interest remaining	$304,423.03
13	principal paid to date	$220.67	interest paid to date	$18,779.33
14	principal this payment	$11.83	interest this payment	$938.17

Constructing the model. Set the column widths as follows:

Column	Width
A	22
B	11
C	27
D	11

- Type in the labels as illustrated in cell ranges A1:A14 and C2:C14.
- Select cells B2 and D2 and format them as percents by choosing Number from the Format menu.
- Select cells B4, B5, B7, B10, B12:B14, D7, D10, and D12:D14, and format these as dollars and cents by choosing Number from the Format menu. (The multiple selection of cells can be accomplished through the use of the Control key.)
- Select cells A1:A5, A7, and A9 and format them as Bold by choosing Fonts from the Format menu.

Figure 4-30. Worksheet with Formulas

	A	B	C	D
1	(Boldface=User Entry)			
2	Interest Rate (annual)		Interest Rate (monthly)	=B2/12
3	Term of Loan (months)			
4	Monthly Payment			
5	Future Value			
6				
7	Present Value	=PV(D2,B3,-B4,-B5)	total amount owed	=(B4*B3)+B5
8				
9	payment #		number of payments remaining	=B3-B9
10	total paid to date	=B9*B4	total of remaining payments	=D7-B10
11				
12	principal remaining	=PV(D2,D9,-B4,-B5)	interest remaining	=D10-B12
13	principal paid to date	=B7-B12	interest paid to date	=B10-B13
14	principal this payment	=PV(D2,D9+1,-B4,-B5)-B12	interest this payment	=B4-B14

• Enter the formulas in their appropriate cells as illustrated:

Cell	Formula
B7	=PV(D2,B3,−B4,−B5)
B10	=B9*B4
B12	=PV(D2,D9,−B4,−B5)
B13	=B7−B12
B14	=PV(D2,D9+1,−B4,−B5)−B12
D2	=B2/12
D7	=(B4*B3)+B5
D9	=B3−B9
D10	=D7−B10
D12	=D10−B12
D13	=B10−B13
D14	=B4−B14

Using the Present Value worksheet. Type in the information that goes in cells B2:B5. This information includes:
• The annual interest rate
• The term (or length) of the loan in months
• The monthly payments
• The future value

The present value will be calculated and displayed in cell
B7. This example is set up as monthly payment periods—if
you wish to use a different payment period, only the formula
in cell D2 need be changed. It currently takes the entered annual interest rate from cell B2 and divides by 12 to find the
monthly interest rate.

If, for example, you wished to change the payment period
from months to years, you would only need to change the formula in cell D2 to =B2 so that cell D2 reflected the annual interest rate. You might also wish to change the labels in cells
C2, A3, and A4 to avoid confusion, although these have no effect on the amounts computed.

The data in cells A9:D14 is meant to show the status of
the loan after a given number of payments. That number can
be entered in cell B9. A complete chart of this information can
be created by adding the formulas and following the instructions from the Loan Amortization worksheet, columns F:I. The
chart transposes perfectly into this worksheet.

Finding Future Value

Figure 4-31. Future Value Worksheet

	A	B	C	D
1	(Boldface=User Entry)			
2	Interest Rate (annual)	12.00%	Interest Rate (monthly)	1.00%
3	Amount of Loan	$100,000.00		
4	Term of Loan (months)	360		
5	Monthly Payment	$900.00		
6				
7	Future Value	$449,496.41	total amount owed	$773,496.41
8				
9	payment #	27	number of payments remaining	333
10	total paid to date	$24,300.00	total of remaining payments	$749,196.41
11				
12	principal remaining	$103,082.09	interest remaining	$646,114.32
13	principal paid to date	($3,082.09)	interest paid to date	$27,382.09
14	principal this payment	($129.53)	interest this payment	$1,029.53

Purpose. Enter the interest rate, amount of the loan, term of the loan, and payment per period, and the worksheet will compute the future value.

One application of future value is for a mortgage buyer to determine how much a balloon payment will be after the term of the mortgage has expired. Or an investor might wish to know how much a piece of property will be worth at a given time in the future if he or she receives x amount of rent and earns y amount of interest.

The worksheet also computes the status of the loan after a given number of payments.

Constructing the model. To create the Future Value spreadsheet:
- Set the column widths as follows:

Column	Width
A	22
B	11
C	27
D	11

- Type in the labels as illustrated in cell ranges A1:A14 and C2:C14.
- Select cells B2 and D2 and format them as percents by choosing Number from the Format menu.
- Select cells B3, B5, B7, B10, B12:B14, D7, D10, and D12:D14, and format these as dollars and cents by choosing Number from the Format menu. (The multiple selection of cells can be accomplished through the use of the Control key.)
- Select cells A1:A5 and A9 and format them as Bold by choosing Fonts from the Format menu.
- Enter the formulas in their appropriate cells as illustrated:

Cell	Formula
B7	=FV(D2,B4,B5,−B3)
B10	=B9*B5
B12	=PV(D2,D9,−B5,−B7)
B13	=B3−B12
B14	=PV(D2,D9+1,−B5,−B7)−B12
D2	=B2/12
D7	=(B4*B5)+B7
D9	=B4−B9

Cell	Formula
D10	=D7−B10
D12	=D10−B12
D13	=B10−B13
D14	=B4−B14

Figure 4-32. Worksheet with Formulas

	A	B	C	D
1	(Boldface=User Entry)			
2	Interest Rate (annual)		Interest Rate (monthly)	=B2/12
3	Amount of Loan			
4	Term of Loan (months)			
5	Monthly Payment			
6				
7	Future Value	=FV(D2,B4,B5,-B3)	total amount owed	=(B4*B5)+B7
8				
9	payment #		number of payments remaining	=B4-B9
10	total paid to date	=B9*B5	total of remaining payments	=D7-B10
11				
12	principal remaining	=PV(D2,D9,-B5,-B7)	interest remaining	=D10-B12
13	principal paid to date	=B3-B12	interest paid to date	=B10-B13
14	principal this payment	=PV(D2,D9+1,-B5,-B7)-B12	interest this payment	=B5-B14

Using the Future Value worksheet. Type in the information that goes in cells B2:B5. This information includes:
• The annual interest rate
• The amount of the loan
• The term (or length) of the loan in months
• The monthly payments

The future value will be computed and displayed in cell B7. This example is set up as monthly payment periods—if you wish to use a different payment period, only the formula in cell D2 need be changed. It currently takes the entered annual interest rate from cell B2 and divides by 12 to find the monthly interest rate.

If, for example, you wished to change the payment period from months to years, you would only need to change the formula in cell D2 to =B2 so that cell D2 reflected the annual interest rate. You might also wish to change the labels in cells C2, A4, and A5 to avoid confusion, although these have no effect on the amounts computed.

The data in cells A9:D14 is meant to show the status of the loan after a given number of payments. That number can be entered in cell B9. A complete chart of this information can be created by adding the formulas and following the instructions from the Loan Amortization worksheet, columns F:I. The chart transposes perfectly into this worksheet.

Finding the Interest Rate

Purpose. Enter the amount of the loan, term of the loan, payment per period, and future value, and the worksheet will compute the interest rate. The worksheet also computes the status of the loan after a given number of payments.

Constructing the model. Set the column widths as follows:

Column	Width
A	22
B	11
C	27
D	11

- Type in the labels as illustrated in cell ranges A1:A14 and C2:C14.
- Select cells B7 and D2 and format them as percents by choosing Number from the Format menu.
- Select cells B2, B4, B5, B10, B12:B14, D7, D10, and D12:D14 and format these as dollars and cents by choosing Number from the Format menu. (The multiple selection of cells can be accomplished through the use of the Control key.)
- Select cells A1:A5 and A9 and format them as bold by choosing Fonts from the Format menu.

Figure 4-33. Interest Rate Worksheet

	A	B	C	D
1	(Boldface=User Entry)			
2	Amount of Loan	$100,000.00	Interest Rate (monthly)	0.90%
3	Term of Loan (months)	360		
4	Monthly Payment	$900.00		
5	Future Value	$100,000.00		
6				
7	Interest Rate (annual)	10.80%	total amount owed	$424,000.00
8				
9	payment #	24	number of payments remaining	336
10	total paid to date	$21,600.00	total of remaining payments	$402,400.00
11				
12	principal remaining	$100,000.00	interest remaining	$302,400.00
13	principal paid to date	$0.00	interest paid to date	$21,600.00
14	principal this payment	$0.00	interest this payment	$900.00

Figure 4-34. Interest Worksheet with Formulas

	A	B	C	D
1	(Boldface=User Entry)			
2	Amount of Loan		Interest Rate (monthly)	=RATE(B3,-B4,B2,-B5,0,0.05)
3	Term of Loan (months)			
4	Monthly Payment			
5	Future Value			
6				
7	Interest Rate (annual)	=D2*12	total amount owed	=(B4*B3)+B5
8				
9	payment #		number of payments remaining	=B3-B9
10	total paid to date	=B9*B4	total of remaining payments	=D7-B10
11				
12	principal remaining	=PV(D2,D9,-B4,-B5)	interest remaining	=D10-B12
13	principal paid to date	=B2-B12	interest paid to date	=B10-B13
14	principal this payment	=PV(D2,D9+1,-B4,-B5)-B12	interest this payment	=B4-B14
15				

• Enter the formulas in their appropriate cells as illustrated:

Cell	Formula
B7	=D2*12
B10	=B9*B4
B12	=PV(D2,D9,−B4,−B5)
B13	=B2−B12
B14	=PV(D2,D9+1,−B4,−B5)−B12
D2	=RATE(B3,−B4,B2,−B5,0,0.05)
D7	=(B4*B3)+B5
D9	=B3−B9
D10	=D7−B10
D12	=D10−B12
D13	=B10−B13
D14	=B4−B14

Using the Interest Rate worksheet. Type in the information that goes in cells B2:B5, including:
• The amount of the loan
• The term (or length) of the loan in months
• The monthly payments
• The future value

The monthly interest rate will be computed and displayed in cell D2. The annual interest rate is computed (monthly times 12) and displayed in cell B7.

In certain cases the interest rate cell and other cells may display *#NUM!* instead of a value. This is caused by the guess, the last number in the formula for cell D2, being too far from the actual interest rate. In the illustrated example, the guess is 5 percent. If you are getting *#NUM!*, try a different value in this formula. Usually a number between 1 percent and 100 percent will provide results, but it may take several tries before you get a successful computation. When in doubt, it is better to guess too high than too low.

The data in cells A9:D14 is meant to show the status of the loan after a given number of payments. That number can be entered in cell B9. A complete chart of this information can be created by adding the formulas and following the instructions from the Loan Amortization worksheet, columns F:I. The chart transposes perfectly into this worksheet.

Loan Amortization

Figure 4-35. The Loan Amortization Worksheet, Columns A–D, Rows 1–14

	A	B	C	D
1	(Boldface=User Entry)			
2	Interest Rate (annual)	12.00%	Interest Rate (monthly)	1.00%
3	Amount of Loan	$100,000.00		
4	Term of Loan (months)	360		
5				
6				
7	Monthly Payment	$1,028.61	total amount owed	$370,300.53
8				
9	payment #	5	number of payments remaining	355
10	total paid to date	$5,143.06	total of remaining payments	$365,157.47
11				
12	principal remaining	$99,854.05	interest remaining	$265,303.42
13	principal paid to date	$145.95	interest paid to date	$4,997.11
14	principal this payment	$29.77	interest this payment	$998.84

Purpose. Enter basic information about a loan (interest rate, amount of the loan, term of the loan) and find out how much the payments come to, how much of a given payment is principal and how much interest, and how much principal remains after a given payment. The worksheet also computes the total amount owed and the total amount of interest paid over the life of the loan.

Figure 4-36. The Worksheet, Columns F–I, Rows 2–18

	F	G	H	I
2	payment #	principal remaining	principal this payment	interest this payment
3	5	$99,854.05	$29.77	$998.84
4	0	$100,000.00	$28.33	$1,000.28
5	1	$99,971.39	$28.61	$1,000.00
6	2	$99,942.49	$28.90	$999.71
7	3	$99,913.30	$29.19	$999.42
8	4	$99,883.82	$29.48	$999.13
9	5	$99,854.05	$29.77	$998.84
10	6	$99,823.97	$30.07	$998.54
11	7	$99,793.60	$30.37	$998.24
12	8	$99,762.93	$30.68	$997.94
13	9	$99,731.94	$30.98	$997.63
14	10	$99,700.65	$31.29	$997.32
15	11	$99,669.04	$31.61	$997.01
16	12	$99,637.12	$31.92	$996.69
17	13	$99,604.88	$32.24	$996.37
18	14	$99,572.32	$32.56	$996.05

Constructing the model. Set the column widths as follows:

Column	Width
A	22
B	11
C	27
D	11
E	10
F	12
G	20
H	22
I	21

Figure 4-37. The Worksheet, Columns F–I, Rows 349–364

	F	G	H	I
349	345	$14,261.77	$877.22	$151.39
350	346	$13,375.77	$885.99	$142.62
351	347	$12,480.92	$894.85	$133.76
352	348	$11,577.11	$903.80	$124.81
353	349	$10,664.27	$912.84	$115.77
354	350	$9,742.30	$921.97	$106.64
355	351	$8,811.11	$931.19	$97.42
356	352	$7,870.61	$940.50	$88.11
357	353	$6,920.71	$949.91	$78.71
358	354	$5,961.30	$959.41	$69.21
359	355	$4,992.30	$969.00	$59.61
360	356	$4,013.61	$978.69	$49.92
361	357	$3,025.13	$988.48	$40.14
362	358	$2,026.77	$998.36	$30.25
363	359	$1,018.43	$1,008.34	$20.27
364	360	$0.00	$1,018.43	$10.18

• Type in the labels as illustrated in cell ranges A1:A14 and C2:C14. Note that the labels in cells F2:I2 are merely references to other cells and need not be typed in.

• Select cells B2 and D2 and format them as percents by choosing Number from the Format menu.

• Select cells B3, B7, B10, B12:B14, D7, D10, D12:D14, and G3:I364, and format these as dollars and cents. (The multiple selection can be accomplished through the use of the Control key and, in the case of G3:I364, the shift key.)

• Select cells A1:A4, A9, and F2:I2 and format them as Bold by choosing Fonts from the Format menu.

Figure 4-38. The Worksheet with Formulas

	A	B	C	D	E	F	G	H	I
1	(Boldface=User Entry)								
2	Interest Rate (annual)		Interest Rate (monthly)	=B2/12		=A9	=A12	=A14	=C14
3	Amount of Loan						=B12	=B14	=D14
4	Term of Loan (months)								
5									
6									
7	Monthly Payment	=PMT(D2,B4,-B3)	total amount owed	=B7*B4					
8									
9	payment #		number of payments remaining	=B4-B9					
10	total paid to date	=B9*B7	total of remaining payments	=D7-B10					
11									
12	principal remaining	=PV(D2,D9,-B7)	interest remaining	=D10-B12					
13	principal paid to date	=B3-B12	interest paid to date	=B10-B13					
14	principal this payment	=PV(D2,D9+1,-B7)-B12	interest this payment	=B7-B14					

- Enter the formulas in their appropriate cells as illustrated:

Cell	Formula
B7	=PMT(D2,B4−B3)
B10	=B9*B7
B12	=PV(D2,D9,−B7)
B13	=B3−B12
B14	=PV(D2,D9+1,−B7)−B12
D2	=B2/12
D7	=B7*B4
D9	=B4−B9
D10	=D7−B10
D12	=D10−B12
D13	=B10−B13
D14	=B7−B14
F2	=A9
G2	=A12
G3	=B12
H2	=A14
H3	=B14
I2	=C14
I3	=D14

You may notice that there are no formulas where the large chart goes; this is because we will use the Table command to create it.

Using the Loan Amortization worksheet. Type in the information that goes in cells B2:B4, including:
- The annual interest rate
- The amount of the loan
- The term (or length) of the loan in months

This example is set up for monthly payments—if the period is different, only the formula in cell D2 need be changed. It currently takes the entered annual interest rate from cell B2 and divides by 12 to find the monthly interest rate.

If, for example, you wished to change the payment period from months to years, you would only need to change the formula in cell D2 to =B2 so that cell D2 reflected the annual interest rate. You might also wish to change the labels in cells C2 and A4 to avoid confusion, although these have no effect on the amounts computed.

The data in cells A9:D14 is meant to show the status of the loan after a given number of payments. That number can be entered in cell B9.

To create a table of the complete loan, we scroll horizontally to view columns F–I. Cells F2:I3 should already be filled in according to their formulas.

- Select cell F4 and type in the number 1.
- With F4 still selected, go to the Series selection on the Data menu. Under Series In, select Columns. Type should be Linear and Step Value should be 1 already. If not, type these in.
- Click the cursor in the Stop Value box and enter the number of periods in your loan (there are 360 in the illustrated example).
- Click OK.
- Column F should fill up with the series of numbers you requested. This could take a while—particularly in the case of 360, so wait until the cursor is no longer an hourglass before continuing.
- Now select cell range F3:I364 if you've chosen 360 periods, or column I and whatever row your numbers extend down to if you've chosen something different.
- From the Data menu, select Table. You will be asked to type in an input cell reference in either the Row or Column box.

• Type B9 in the Column box to indicate that the numbers in column F will replace the input value in cell B9. You will then see your table fill in slowly—again, if you have 360 rows to fill in, this could take a while. Your cursor will appear as an hourglass shape until it is done.

Finally, you may wish to enter the formula =B9 in cell F3 to indicate what payment number row 3 is referring to. This was left until last because that value would have confused the program when the table was being created.

Data Processing

Templates covered in this section include:
• Mailing list
• Finding and extracting from a database

Mailing List

Purpose. Provides sorting (including that done by zip code) and alphabetizing of a lengthy mailing list, which can later be printed out to make mailing labels or individual addresses on envelopes.

   Constructing the model. This is probably one of the easiest models to construct. Column widths can be set for any convenient width and later expanded if necessary; in the example they are set as follows:

Column	Width
A	16
B	16
C	16
D	25
E	16
F	7
G	7

Labels are typed into A1:G1—feel free to alter or combine fields according to your own needs. Keep in mind that any sorting or searching will be done by fields or discrete columns; therefore it would be difficult, for example, to sort by street names in the illustrated example because they are combined

Figure 4-39. The Database Worksheet

	A	B	C	D	E	F	G
2	LAST	FIRST	COMPANY	STREET	CITY	STATE	ZIP
3	Anders	Kenley	Coit Plumbing	3434 Tract Twentyfour	El Toro	CA	92346
4	Cattory	Palmer	Tropical Fish Inc.	5603 Orange Grove Ave.	West Hollywood	CA	90046
5	Hatter	Guy	You-Too Entertain.	1212 Colosseum Way	Los Angeles	CA	90021
6	Leah	Patrick	Patrick Paints It	78543 Diedre Lane	Simi Valley	CA	90427
7	McEnery	Kelbe	Answer Service	220 Coral Pl.	Vista	CA	92501
8	Millen	Denny	Southwest Models	4310 Grandier St.	Burbank	CA	91505
9	Mullady	Mary Anne	Sober Escort Srv.	250 Mariposa St.	Burbank	CA	91506
10	Redford	Yogi	Filet Mignon Assn.	5134 Valley St. #5	Beverly Hills	CA	90145
11	Woodward	Cookie	Complaint Dept.	825 N. Keyhole St.	Burbank	CA	91506
12	Wyzel	Allen	Tarzana Dental	18372 Burbank Blvd.	Tarzana	CA	91356

with street numbers. Zip codes are given their own field since post offices often offer discounts for mail that has been presorted by zip code.

After the headings are typed in, centered, and boldfaced (the latter two done from the Format menu), the model is completed.

Using the model. Although the illustrated example contains a short mailing list, the advantage of *Excel* lies in large, otherwise unmanageable mailing lists. Whereas other database programs might require much trouble and complication to change the size of a field, if you run into a longer name than usual, in *Excel* you simply move the column over. Do likewise for inserting or deleting fields (columns).

The first process to go through when the list is to be used is as follows:

• Select the entire list, either by starting the cursor at A3 and dragging it down to the bottom right, or, if the list is too long, selecting A3, and with the shift key down, selecting the bottom right cell. All other cells in between will then be selected.

• Now we want to name this selection so that in the future we can use the Formula menu's Goto function.

• Select Define Name from the Formula menu. We named ours *MAILLIST*.

- Once this selection is named, you can test the function by selecting a cell at random, then using Goto on the Formula menu. When you double-click your list's name, the entire list should be selected.
- *Excel* offers a form for entering data—some people find this easier than using the spreadsheet. After the fields have been named and the database defined, select Form from the Data menu.

  Let's begin by alphabetizing the list.
- Select the entire list; then choose Sort in the Data menu. Probably the first key will read *$A$3* (if not, type this in). If they have not already been selected, choose Rows and Ascending.
- Fill in the second key as *$B$3*. This means that if the last names are the same, *Excel* will go to the first names to alphabetize.
- Click OK. Your list will be alphabetized.

  Let's sort by zip code.
- Again choose Sort from the Data menu. This time make *$G$3* the first key choice, *$A$3* the second key choice, and *$B$3* the third key choice. Be sure not to type Enter until all three are filled in. Now the list is sorted first by zip code, then by last name, then by first name.

  You can put 16,383 names on this list. If that's not enough, you can start another list next to the original one, putting A–L on one list and M–Z on another.

  In addition to sorting, finding and extracting are also possible.These are accomplished with the database functions, and are covered in the next section.

Finding and Extracting from a Database

Purpose. An *Excel* database can be sorted in very specific ways, to meet certain narrow or broad criteria. The matching records can be found, extracted, deleted, or altered. For the purpose of our example, we will continue using the mailing list begun in Figure 4-39. The list in the example is short; keep

Figure 4-40. A Database Example

	A	B	C	D	E	F	G
2	LAST	FIRST	COMPANY	STREET	CITY	STATE	ZIP
3	Anders	Kenley	Coit Plumbing	3434 Tract Twentyfour	El Toro	CA	92348
4	Cattory	Palmer	Tropical Fish Inc.	5603 Orange Grove Ave.	West Hollywood	CA	90046
5	Hatter	Guy	You-Too Entertain.	1212 Colosseum Way	Los Angeles	CA	90021
6	Leah	Patrick	Patrick Paints It	78543 Diedre Lane	Simi Valley	CA	90427
7	McEnery	Kelbe	Answer Service	220 Coral Pl.	Vista	CA	92501
8	Millen	Denny	Southwest Models	4310 Grandler St.	Burbank	CA	91505
9	Mullady	Mary Anne	Sober Escort Srv.	250 Mariposa St.	Burbank	CA	91506
10	Redford	Yogi	Filet Mignon Assn.	5134 Valley St. #5	Beverly Hills	CA	90145
11	Woodward	Cookie	Complaint Dept.	825 N. Keyhole St.	Burbank	CA	91506
12	Wyzel	Allen	Tarzana Dental	18372 Burbank Blvd.	Tarzana	CA	91356
13							
14							
15	LAST	FIRST	COMPANY	STREET	CITY	STATE	ZIP
16	>Mcf	>A					
17							
18	LAST	FIRST	COMPANY	STREET	CITY	STATE	ZIP
19	Millen	Denny	Southwest Models	4310 Grandler St.	Burbank	CA	91505
20	Mullady	Mary Anne	Sober Escort Srv.	250 Mariposa St.	Burbank	CA	91506
21	Redford	Yogi	Filet Mignon Assn.	5134 Valley St. #5	Beverly Hills	CA	90145
22	Woodward	Cookie	Complaint Dept.	825 N. Keyhole St.	Burbank	CA	91506
23	Wyzel	Allen	Tarzana Dental	18372 Burbank Blvd.	Tarzana	CA	91356

in mind that the database functions would be most useful on long and cumbersome lists.

Constructing the model. We will build on the model created for the previous example, MAILLIST.
- Select cells A2:G2, which comprise the headings. These will be copied and pasted twice.
- Select Copy from the Edit menu, and then select cell A15. (If your list is longer than the example's, choose a cell a few rows below the last name on the list. Be sure to convert the following references to your new location.)
- Choose Paste from the Edit menu.
- Now select cell A18 and choose Paste again. The headings should be duplicated twice as in the illustrated example.

We will now define the database:
- Select your entire list (cells A3:G12 in the example) and choose Set Database from the Data menu.

- Now select the headings at the bottom (A18:G18 in the example) and choose Define Name from the Formula menu. Name this range of cells *Ext* for extract.

Using Database. What can Database do that Sort in the previous section couldn't? Let's start with a simple example. Suppose we were looking for all the names on the list that begin with the letter *S*. Using Sort we could alphabetize the whole list, scroll through until we found the S's, define the records, copy them, and paste them somewhere else. That's the hard way.

The easy way is with a database criteria function. Under the heading LAST, in cell A16, we will type the letter *S*. This tells *Excel* to find all records with a last name beginning with *S*. (If we typed *Sm* in this cell, *Excel* would find all records beginning with *Sm*, such as Smith and Smedley.) We must define the criteria range before the sort and extraction can take place. In other words, we must tell *Excel* that we are only concerned with last names and only the letter *S*. To do this:

- Select cells A15 and A16 and choose Set Criteria from the Data menu. Now *Excel* knows exactly what is included in the criteria.
- Next we must tell *Excel* where to place the extracted records. From the Formula menu, select Goto and double-click Ext, which is how we defined the bottom headings. Now we are ready for the search and extraction to commence.
- Select Extract from the Data menu. If there are duplicate records in your list, you might want to check Unique Records Only to avoid duplicates in the list.
- Click OK. Under the headings, beginning in row 19 (in the example), all records beginning with *S* will be listed.

Let's try a more complicated search. We want to find all records with last names that begin with a letter higher than the letter *K*. Of those, we want only the records with first names that are higher than the letter *C*.

- In cell A16 under LAST we enter >L (higher than *K*). All comparison operators can be used in this context (=, >, <, <=, >=, < >). But why did we choose *L* when we wanted

higher than *K*? Because *Excel* is very literal-minded—it considers *La* higher than *L*. We could have said >*Kz*, but we are assuming that there are no last names that simply consist of L.
- Now, in cell B16 we enter >D to indicate that a match consists of any first name beginning with *Da* or something further along in the alphabet (such as *Denny*).

Now we redefine the criteria area.
- Choose Set Criteria from the Data menu.
- Next we tell *Excel* where to place the extracted names by choosing Goto from the Formula menu and selecting Ext.
- Finally, we select Extract from the Data menu. The records meeting the new criteria will list below the headings.

A few details: The criteria area must be a continuous selection, meaning that if you want to specify a last name and a zip code, you must put these two headings next to each other and select them together. You're even allowed to use the same heading twice for two criteria in the same field. In the extracted section, you don't have to list the field headings in the same order as was used in the database, and you don't have to include all of them. You can repeat them more than once. The records will appear in the format you have arranged for the headings.

Obviously, we have only scratched the surface of what the database search function can do. You could, for example, find records of people within a certain area who spent more than a given amount with your company, provided that you included sales figures in the database. You could even concoct complex formulas as criteria, such as sorting only records where the quantity of items times the price of items is more than a certain amount. In addition to extracting records, you could delete records matching the criteria as well as merely finding those records.

Appendices

Appendix A
Quick-Reference Command Chart

A quick-reference command chart of the main *Excel* commands is given below, with the commands listed in menu order.

To execute the commands below:
- Press the Alt key and release.
- Press the underlined letter of the menu that the command is on, and release.
- Press the underlined letter of the command and release.

Exceptions to the instructions above are the commands on the Control menu. To execute those commands:
- Press the Alt key and release.
- Press either the space bar or the hyphen key (depending on whether you want the document or application menu) and release.
- Press the underlined letter of the command and release.

The other exceptions are the commands which bypass the menu; these do not have an underlined letter and are executed by pressing the indicated key(s).

Some keyboard shortcuts are available which reduce the number of keystrokes necessary to complete a command. These are in the third column. If the keys are separated by a plus sign, that means to press the keys simultaneously.

Command	Worksheet Menu	Keyboard Shortcut
Restore	Control Menu	Control + F5 (Document)
		Alt + F5 (Application)
Move	Control Menu	Control + F7 (Document)
		Alt + F7 (Application)
Size	Control Menu	Control + F8 (Document)
		Alt + F8 (Application)

Command	Worksheet Menu	Keyboard Shortcut
Maximize	Control Menu	Control + F10 (Document)
		Alt + F10 (Application)
Minimize	Control Menu	Alt + F9 (Application)
Close	Control Menu	Control + F4 (Document)
		Alt + F4 (Application)
Run	Control Menu	
Split	Control Menu	
New	File Menu	Alt + F1 (Chart)
		Alt + Shift + F1 (Worksheet)
		Alt + Ctrl + F1 (Macro)
Open	File Menu	Alt + Ctrl + F2
Close	File Menu	
Links	File Menu	
Save	File Menu	Alt + Shift + F2
Save As	File Menu	Alt + F2
Delete	File Menu	
Page Setup	File Menu	
Print	File Menu	Alt + Ctrl + Shift + F2
Printer Setup	File Menu	
Exit	File Menu	
Undo	Edit Menu	
Repeat	Edit Menu	
Cut	Edit Menu	Shift + Delete
Copy	Edit Menu	Control + Insert
Paste	Edit Menu	Shift + Insert
Clear	Edit Menu	Del
Paste Special	Edit Menu	
Paste Link	Edit Menu	
Delete	Edit Menu	
Insert	Edit Menu	
Fill Right	Edit Menu	
Fill Down	Edit Menu	
Activate Formula Bar		F2
Extend Toggle		F8
Add		Shift + F8
Paste Name	Formula Menu	F3
Paste Function	Formula Menu	Shift + F3
Reference	Formula Menu	F4
Define Name	Formula Menu	Control + F3
Create Names	Formula Menu	Control + Shift + F3
Apply Names	Formula Menu	
Note	Formula Menu	Shift + F2
Goto	Formula Menu	F5

Command	Worksheet Menu	Keyboard Shortcut
Find	Formula Menu	Shift + F5
		F7 (Find next cell)
		Shift + F7 (Find previous cell)
Replace	Formula Menu	
Select Special	Formula Menu	Ctrl + ? * / \ ! [ ] { }
Number	Format Menu	Ctrl + ! @ # $ % ^
Alignment	Format Menu	
Font	Format Menu	Ctrl + 1 2 3 4
Border	Format Menu	
Cell Protection	Format Menu	
Row Height	Format Menu	
Column Width	Format Menu	
Justify	Format Menu	
Form	Data Menu	
Find	Data Menu	
Extract	Data Menu	
Delete	Data Menu	
Set Database	Data Menu	
Set Criteria	Data Menu	
Sort	Data Menu	
Series	Data Menu	
Table	Data Menu	
Parse	Data Menu	
Set Print Area	Options Menu	
Set Print Titles	Options Menu	
Set Page Break	Options Menu	
Display	Options Menu	Ctrl + ' (Formulas/values toggle)
Freeze Panes	Options Menu	
Protect Document	Options Menu	
Calculation	Options Menu	
Calculate Now	Options Menu	Shift + F9 *or* Ctrl + =
Calculate Document	Options Menu	F9
Workspace	Options Menu	
Short Menus	Options Menu	
Record	Macro Menu	
Run	Macro Menu	
Start Recorder	Macro Menu	
Set Recorder	Macro Menu	
Relative record	Macro Menu	
New Window	Window Menu	
Show Info	Window Menu	Shift + F2
Arrange All	Window Menu	
Hide	Window Menu	

Quick
Commands

185

Command	Worksheet Menu	Keyboard Shortcut
Unhide	Window Menu	
1 Sheet1.XLS	Window Menu	
Next Pane		F6
Previous Pane		Shift + F6
Next Document Window		Control + F6
Previous Document Window		Control + Shift + F6
Index	Help Menu	F1 (Help)
		Shift + F1 (Context-sensitive help)
Keyboard	Help Menu	
Lotus 123	Help Menu	
Multiplan	Help Menu	
Tutorial	Help Menu	
Feature Guide	Help Menu	
About	Help Menu	

Appendix B
Function List

ABS(number)
Purpose: Mathematical
Meaning: Returns the absolute value of a number.
Example: ABS(3) = 3
Example: ABS(−3) = 3

ACOS(number)
Purpose: Trigonometric
Meaning: Returns the arccosine of a number.
Example: ACOS(0.7) = 0.795399

AND(logicals1,logicals2, . . .)
Purpose: Logical
Meaning: Returns TRUE if all values are true; otherwise returns FALSE.
Example: AND(2*3=6,2−1=1) = TRUE
Example: AND(2*3=6,2−1=0) = FALSE

AREAS(ref)
Purpose: Special Purpose
Meaning: Returns the number of areas (continuous ranges of cells).
Example: AREAS(C1:D4,F3,G6:H8) = 3
Example: AREAS(C1:D4) = 1

ASIN(number)
Purpose: Trigonometric
Meaning: Returns the arcsine of a number.
Example: ASIN(.7) = 0.775397

ATAN(number)
Purpose: Trigonometric
Meaning: Returns the arctangent of a number.
Example: ATAN(.7) = 0.610726

ATAN2(x-number,y-number)
Purpose: Trigonometric
Meaning: Returns the arctagent of two numbers.
Example: ATAN2(.7,.7) = 0.785398

AVERAGE(numbers-1,numbers-2, . . .)
Purpose: Statistical
Meaning: Returns the average of a list of numbers.
Example: AVERAGE(2,4,6,8,10) = 6

CHOOSE(index,value-1,value-2, . . .)
Purpose: Logical
Meaning: Returns the indexed value of a list.
Example: CHOOSE(3,"First","Second","Third","Fourth")
         = "Third"

COLUMN(ref)
Purpose: Special Purpose
Meaning: Returns the column number of the referenced cell
         or cells. More than one column returns as an
         array.
Example: COLUMN(A1:D4) = {1,2,3,4}

COLUMNS(array)
Purpose: Special Purpose
Meaning: Returns the number of columns in an array.
Example: COLUMNS({1,2,3;4,5,6}) = 3

COS(number)
Purpose: Trigonometric
Meaning: Returns the cosine of a number.
Example: COS(.7) = 0.764842

COUNT(numbers-1,numbers-2, . . .)
Purpose: Statistical
Meaning: Returns the count of the numbers in the list.
Example: COUNT(1,3,16,78,4) = 5

DATE(year,month,day)

Purpose: Date

Meaning: Returns the serial number of the date (the number of days since January 1, 1904), given in "(year,month,day)" format.

Example: DATE(1985,3,1) = 31107

DAVERAGE(database,field-name,criteria)

Purpose: Database

Meaning: Returns the average of the numbers in a particular field of a database that meet the criteria supplied in the form of a cell range reference.

Example: DAVERAGE(Database,Sale_total,A1:B2) = 450.24

DAY(serial-number)

MONTH(serial-number)

YEAR(serial-number)

WEEKDAY(serial-number)

Purpose: Date

Meaning: Returns a day, month, year, or weekday from a supplied serial number. An accepted date format may also be supplied.

Example: WEEKDAY("3/1/85") = 6 (or Friday)

DCOUNT(database,field-name,criteria)

Purpose: Database

Meaning: Returns the count of the numbers from a field in a database that satisfy a particular criterion.

Example: DCOUNT(Database,Total_Sales,A1:B2) = 26

DMAX(database,field-name,criteria)

Purpose: Database

Meaning: Returns the largest number from the numbers in a specified database field that satisfy a particular criterion.

Example: DMAX(Database,Total_Sales,A1:B2) = 1225.80

Function
Summary

189

DMIN(database,field-name,criteria)
Purpose: Database
Meaning: Returns the smallest number from the numbers in a specified database field that satisfy a particular criterion.
Example: DMIN( )(Database,Total_Sales,A1:B2) = 101.50

DOLLAR(number,number of digits)
Purpose: Text
Meaning: Returns a rounded number to the specified number of digits, in text format.
Example: DOLLAR(1245.6798,2) = "$1245.68"

DSTDEV(database,field-name,criteria)
Purpose: Database/Statistical
Meaning: Returns the standard deviation of the numbers in a specified field of a database that satisfy a specified criterion.
Example: DSTDEV(Database,Total_Sales,A1:B2) = 24

DSUM(database,fieldname,criteria)
Purpose: Database
Meaning: Returns the sum of the numbers in a specified field of a database that satisfy a specified criterion.
Example: DSUM(Database,Total_Sales,A1:B2) = 10,843.60

DVAR(database,fieldname,criteria)
Purpose: Database/Statistical
Meaning: Returns the sample variance from the numbers in a specified field of a database that satisfy a specified criterion.
Example: DVAR(Database,Total_Sales,A1:B2) = 1.2

EXP(number)
Purpose: Mathematical
Meaning: Returns *e* (2.7182818 . . .) raised to the power of the supplied number.
Example: EXP(1) = 2.7182818

FALSE( )

Purpose: Logical

Meaning: Returns the logical value of FALSE.

Example: FALSE( ) = FALSE

FIXED(number,number of digits)

Purpose: Text

Meaning: Returns, in text format, a number rounded to a specified number of digits from a supplied number.

Example: FIXED(1245.678,2) = "1245.68"

FV(rate,nper,pmt,pv,type)

Purpose: Financial

Meaning: Returns the future value of an investment from specified rate, number of periods, payment, present value, type. *See* PV( )

GROWTH(Y-array,X-array,x-array)

Purpose: Statistical

Meaning: Returns, as an array, the *y* values on the exponential curve of regression for two variables.

HLOOKUP(lookup value,compare array,index number)

VLOOKUP(lookup value,compare array,index number)

Purpose: Special Purpose

Meaning: Searches a specified array for a specified lookup value, then proceeds down the found column (VLOOKUP) or across the found row (HLOOKUP) the number of cells specified. The value need not match exactly. The search will halt at the largest value that is less than or equal to the lookup amount.

Example: HLOOKUP(20000,A1:F8,3) = 35

HOUR(serial number)

MINUTE(serial number)

Function Summary

SECOND(serial number)
Purpose: Date
Meaning: Returns the hour (on the 24-hour clock), minute, or second from a supplied serial number.
Example: HOUR(0.7) = 16

IF(logical,value if true,value if false)
Purpose: Logical
Meaning: Returns one specified value if supplied equation is true, and another specified value if it is false.
Example: IF(2+3=6,"Yes","No") = "No"

INDEX(ref,row,column,area)
Purpose: Special Purpose
Meaning: Returns the value of a cell in specified range(s), with specified row and column indices pointing the way. If more than one cell range is supplied, a specified area index will point to the range. If only one range is supplied, or an array is supplied, the area index is not necessary.
Example: INDEX((A1:C3,D5:F8),2,4,1) = 45

INT(number)
Purpose: Mathematical
Meaning: Returns the largest integer less than or equal to the supplied number.
Example: INT(5.9) = 5
Example: INT(−5.9) = −6

IRR(values,guess)
Purpose: Financial
Meaning: Returns the internal rate of return from a series of supplied cash flows. Iteration is used to find the value. An optional guess may be supplied, giving the starting value of the iteration. An error value returns (#NUM!) if, after 20 iterations, the value does not converge to within .0000001.
Example: IRR(−1000,1000,1500,2000,−3000,−4000, 5000, 70%) = 0.816753

ISERROR(value)

Purpose: Logical

Meaning: Returns TRUE if an error message results because of supplied value; returns FALSE otherwise.

Example: ISERROR(3/0) = TRUE

ISNA(value)

Purpose: Logical

Meaning: Returns TRUE if value produces the error message #N/A (not available). Otherwise, returns FALSE.

Example: ISNA(Unopened!A1) = TRUE (if "Unopened" is an unopened worksheet)

ISREF(value)

Purpose: Logical

Meaning: Returns TRUE if the supplied value is a reference or a reference formula. Otherwise, returns FALSE.

Example: ISREF(B1) = TRUE

Example: ISREF(B1+D2) = FALSE

LEN(text)

Purpose: Text

Meaning: Returns the length, in number of characters, of a text string.

Example: LEN("Hello I love you") = 16

LINEST(Y-array,X-array)

Purpose: Statistical

Meaning: Returns as a horizontal array of two elements the slope and y-intercept of the line of regression for two random variables supplied as two arrays.

Example: LINEST(C1:G1,{1,2,3,4,5}) = {2000,3000}

LN(number)

Purpose: Mathematical

Meaning: Returns the natural logarithm of a supplied number.

Example: LN(2.7182818) = 1

LOG10(number)
Purpose: Mathematical
Meaning: Returns the base 10 logarithm of a supplied
number.
Example: LOG10(10)_ = 1

LOGEST(Y-array,X-array)
Purpose: Statistical
Meaning: Returns, as a horizontal array of two elements,
the parameters m and b of the exponential curve
of regression $y = b * m \, ^\wedge x$, for two variables, x
and y, represented by x array and y array.
Example: LOGEST(A1:A3,B1:B3) = 0.57735 (where A1:A3
contains 1,2,3 and B1:B3 contains 3,2,1)

LOOKUP(lookup value,compare vector,result vector)
Purpose: Special Purpose
Meaning: Searches the compare vector for the largest value
equal to or less than the lookup value, then returns the value in the result vector that corresponds in position to the cell found in the
compare vector. The values in the compare vector
must be in ascending order, and can be numbers,
text, or logical values.
Example: LOOKUP(27,A1:C1,A2:C2) = "One-quarter"
(where A1:C1 contains 10,25,33 and A2:C2 contains "One-tenth","One-quarter", and "One-
third")

For users of *Multiplan*, the Lookup function can also be
used in the form LOOKUP(lookup value,compare array).

MATCH(lookup value,compare vector,type)
Purpose: Special Purpose
Meaning: Returns the sequential number position of the
lookup value within the compare vector. If type is
1, the largest comparison value that is less than
or equal to the lookup value is matched. If type is
-1, the smallest compare vector value that is
greater than or equal to the lookup value is
matched. If type is 0, only a perfect match will return a value other than #N/A.

Example: MATCH(20,A1:C1,0) = 2 (where A1:C1 contains 10,20,30)

MAX(number1,number2, . . .)
Purpose: Statistical
Meaning: Returns the largest number in the list of supplied numbers.
Example: MAX(2,8,23,7,4) = 23

MID(text,start-position,number of characters)
Purpose: Text
Meaning: Returns the number of characters that are extracted from the supplied text, starting at the start position.
Example: MID("Hiya Hollywood, Hiya",6,5) = "Holly"

MIN(numbers-1,numbers-2, . . .)
Purpose: Statistical
Meaning: Returns the smallest number in the list of supplied numbers.
Example: MIN(2,8,23,7,4) = 2

MINUTE(serial number)
See HOUR.

MIRR(values,safe,risk)
Purpose: Financial
Meaning: Returns the modified internal rate of return of a series of cashflows (values). Safe represents the rate returned that will finance negative cashflow, and risk represents the rate at which positive cashflow can be reinvested.
Example: MIRR($-$1000,1000,1500,2000,$-$3000,$-$4000, 5000,70%,75%) = 0.744188

MOD(number,divisor-number)
Purpose: Mathematical
Meaning: Returns the modulus (or remainder) of the division: number/divisor.
Example: MOD(5,3) = 2

Function Summary

MONTH(serial number)
See DAY.

NA( )
Purpose: Special Purpose
Meaning: Returns the error value #N/A.
Example: NA( ) = #N/A (error value)

NOT(logical)
Purpose: Logical
Meaning: Returns the opposite logical value of the logical statement supplied.
Example: NOT(2*4=8) = FALSE
Example: NOT(2*4=9) = TRUE

NOW( )
Purpose: Date
Meaning: Returns the serial number of the current date and time. This number is updated at every recalculation. The serial number can be converted into a given format by placing this function in a formatted cell.
Example: NOW( ) = 12/21/87 18:46

NPER(rate,pmt,pv,fv,type)
Purpose: Financial
Meaning: Returns the number of periods for the supplied rate, payment amount, present value, future value, and type. See PV( ).

NPV(rate,values-1,values-2, . . .)
Purpose: Financial
Meaning: Returns the net present value for a series of future cashflows (values), discounted at a constant rate of interest (rate).
Example: NPV(15%,2000,4000,8000) = 10023.83

OR(logical1,logical2, . . .)
Purpose: Logical
Meaning: Returns TRUE if any of the supplied logical values are true; otherwise returns FALSE.

Example: OR(2*4=7,2*4=8) = TRUE
Example: OR(2*4=7,2*4=9) = FALSE

PI( )

Purpose: Mathematical
Meaning: Returns 3.14159 . . ., the mathematical constant
pi.

PMT(rate,nper,pv,fv,type)

Purpose: Financial
Meaning: Returns the payment amount for supplied interest
rate, number of periods, present value, future
value, and type. See PV( ).

PV(rate,nper,pmt,fv,type)

FV(rate,nper,pmt,pv,type)

NPER(rate,pmt,pv,fv,type)

PMT(rate,nper,pv,fv,type)

RATE(nper,pmt,pv,fv,type,guess)

Purpose: Financial
Meaning: Each returns its title, given the other variables in
a constant cashflow equation. For example, PV
(present value) is returned when the interest rate,
number of periods, payment amount, future
value, and type are supplied. Type refers to
whether the payments come at the beginning or
at the end of the period. Type 0 indicates payments come at the end, the first payment coming
at the end of the first period. Type 1 indicates the
the payments come at the beginning of the periods. Since rate is solved by iteration, a guess can
be supplied, which reduces the number of iterations. Cash received is a positive number; cash
paid out is a negative number.
Example: PV(18%,12,−112,−4000,0) = 1085.719285

Function
Summary

RAND( )
Purpose: Mathematical
Meaning: Returns a random number in the range 0 to
.9999 . . . . A new number is generated every time
the sheet is recalculated.
Example: RAND( ) = .5643

RATE(nper,pmt,pv,fv,type,guess)
Purpose: Financial
Meaning: Returns the interest rate when the number of periods, payment amount, present value, future
value, and type are supplied. Guess is an optional
starting point for the iterations. See PV( ).

REPT(text,number of times)
Purpose: Text
Meaning: Returns a text value that repeats the supplied text
the specified number of times.
Example: REPT(":*",5) = ":*:*:*:*:*"

ROUND(number,number of digits)
Purpose: Mathematical
Meaning: Returns a number rounded off to the number of
digits specified. If that number is 0, an integer is
returned. If that number is negative, the supplied
number is rounded that many places to the left of
the decimal point.
Example: ROUND(123.456,2) = 123.46
Example: ROUND(123.456,0) = 123
Example: ROUND(123.456,−2) = 100

ROW(ref)
Purpose: Special Purpose
Meaning: Returns the row number of the reference, if the
reference is a single cell. If the reference is a
range of cells, the row numbers are returned as a
vertical array.
Example: ROW(A1:B3) = {1;2;3}

ROWS(array)

Purpose: Special Purpose
Meaning: Returns the number of rows in the supplied array.
Example: ROWS(A1:B3) = 3

SEARCH(search-text,text,start number)

Purpose: Text
Meaning: Returns the number, in character count, at which the search text appears in text. The start number is the number, in character count, where the search should begin. Wild cards may be used (that is, the asterisk and question mark can be used to stand for a series of trailing characters or a single character, respectively), and case is ignored.
Example: SEARCH("-","nicely-tanned",1) = 7

SECOND(serial number)

Purpose: Date
Meaning: Returns the second from the supplied serial number. *See* HOUR( ).

SIGN(number)

Purpose: Mathematical
Meaning: Returns 1 if the supplied number is positive, -1 if the number is negative, and 0 if the number is 0.
Example: SIGN(4*3) = 1
Example: SIGN(4*-3) = -1
Example: SIGN(4*0) = 0

SIN(number)

Purpose: Trigonometric
Meaning: Returns the sine of a supplied number.
Example: SIN(1.5) = 0.997495

SQRT(number)

Purpose: Mathematical
Meaning: Returns the square root of a supplied number.
Example: SQRT(4) = 2

Function
Summary

STDEV(number1,number2, . . .)
   Purpose: Statistical
   Meaning: Returns the standard deviation of the numbers
             supplied.
   Example: STDEV(1,4,3,6,9) = 3.04959

SUM(numbers-1,numbers-2, . . .)
   Purpose: Mathematical
   Meaning: Returns the sum of the numbers supplied.
   Example: SUM(2,4,6,8) = 20

TAN(number)
   Purpose: Trigonometric
   Meaning: Returns the tangent of the number supplied,
             given in radians.
   Example: TAN(1.5) = 14.10142

TEXT(number,format-text)
   Purpose: Text
   Meaning: Converts a number into text in the format
             specified.
   Example: TEXT(4.789,"$0.00") = "$4.79"

TIME(hour,minute,second)
   Purpose: Date
   Meaning: Returns the serial number of the time specified.
   Example: TIME(12,24,36) = 0.517083

TRANSPOSE(array)
   Purpose: Mathematical
   Meaning: Returns an array that is the transposition of the
             supplied array.
   Example: TRANSPOSE({1,2,3;4,5,6}) = {1,4;2,5;3,6}

TREND(Y-array,X-array,x-array)
   Purpose: Statistical
   Meaning: Returns the y values on the line of regression, y
             $= mx + b$, for two random variables, X and Y (X-
             array and Y-array).
   Example: TREND(A1:D1,{1,2,3,4}) = 800 (where A1:D1
             holds 1000,1500,3000,4000)

TRUE( )
  Purpose: Logical
  Meaning: Returns the logical value TRUE
  Example: TRUE( ) = TRUE

TYPE(value)
  Purpose: Special Purpose
  Meaning: Returns the type of value supplied. If the value is
           a number, TYPE( ) returns 1, text = 2, logi-
           cal = 4, error value = 16, array = 64. The table
           below shows the values returned for the various
           types of values.
  Example: TYPE({1,2,3;4,5,6}) = 64

VALUE(text)
  Purpose: Text
  Meaning: Returns a number from supplied text.
  Example: VALUE("$45.67") = 45.67

VAR(numbers-1,numbers-2, . . .)
  Purpose: Statistical
  Meaning: Returns the simple variance of the numbers
           supplied.
  Example: VAR(2,4,6,8,10) = 10

VLOOKUP(lookup value,compare array,index number)
See HLOOKUP.

WEEKDAY(serial number)
See DAY.

YEAR(serial number)
See DAY.

Function
Summary

Appendix C
Interfacing with Other Software

Although *Excel* is a self-contained program, there may be instances where you'll need to interface with other software. *Excel* has anticipated this need, and has provided means to transfer data and graphics from itself to other software, as well as to import data from certain spreadsheet, database, and word processing files.

Let's begin with the options on the Save As command from the File menu. If you choose Options, a dialog box appears listing the various formats in which your worksheet can be saved. These options allow various other software programs to read your *Excel* file.

- *Normal* is the format *Excel* uses, and is the default choice.
- *Text* is used to transfer data to a word processor. Only text and values are saved—underlying formulas are discarded. This option creates an ASCII file in which the *Excel* spreadsheet columns are separated by tabs, and the rows are separated by carriage returns. If a cell contains a comma or a tab, it is enclosed in quotation marks in the new text file.
- *CSV* stands for comma-separated values, and is similar to the text format, except that columns are separated by commas rather than by tabs. Just as in the text format, commas in a cell are surrounded by quotation marks.
- *SYLK* is used to export data to another Microsoft spreadsheet such as *Multiplan* or *Excel* for the Apple Macintosh.
- *WKS* transfers data to *Lotus 1-2-3*, version 1A, or *Symphony* on the IBM PC.
- *WK1* transfers data to *Lotus 1-2-3*, version 2, on the IBM PC.
- *DIF* is used to transfer data to a program that requires Data Interchange Format. *VisiCalc* is one example of such a program. Like Text and CSV, DIF does not save formulas, but only the values produced by them.

- *DBF* 2 allows the export of a database range on your *Excel* worksheet to *dBase II*.
- *DBF* 3 allows the export of a database range on your *Excel* worksheet to *dBase III*.

Just as all these formats can be exported with the use of these options, so too can they be imported. *Excel* automatically recognizes the format being read and makes the conversion. There is a macro conversion program included with *Excel* that allows *Lotus 1-2-3* macros to be converted to *Excel* macros.

Excel can also transfer its charts and spreadsheets into another Windows application, such as *Write*. You need Windows 2.0 or higher to use this feature. *Excel* transfers whatever you specify to the Clipboard when you select cells or a chart and then immediately exit the program. You may either switch away from the *Excel* window or close the *Excel* window. In either case, the selection is copied to the Clipboard and can be pasted using the receiving application's Paste command.

The data is converted to a form the receiving program can handle. If the receiving program is not a standard Windows application, certain limited transferring can still take place. The Paste option on the Windows menu is utilized in this case. Whether the transfer can take place or not depends on the receiving program. The best way to find out what kinds of data can be transferred is simply to try it.

Index

COMPUTE! Books

Ask your retailer for these **COMPUTE! Books** or order directly from **COMPUTE!**.

Write COMPUTE! Books, F.D.R. Station, P.O. Box 5038, New York, NY 10150.

Quantity	Title	Price*	Total
_____	COMPUTE!'s Quick and Easy Guide to Using MS-DOS (105-6)	**$12.95**	_____
_____	COMPUTE!'s Quick and Easy Guide to Learning Lotus 1-2-3 (106-4)	**$12.95**	_____
_____	COMPUTE!'s Quick and Easy Guide to AppleWorks (109-9)	**$10.95**	_____
_____	COMPUTE!'s Quick and Easy Guide to dBase III Plus (107-2)	**$10.95**	_____
_____	COMPUTE!'s Quick and Easy Guide to WordPerfect (011-4)	**$10.95**	_____
_____	COMPUTE!'s Quick and Easy Guide to Desktop Publishing (112-9)	**$10.95**	_____
_____	COMPUTE!'s Quick and Easy Guide to Dow Jones News/Retrieval (113-7)	**$10.95**	_____
_____	COMPUTE!'s Quick & Easy Guide to Microsoft Word on the IBM (133-1)	**$10.95**	_____
_____	COMPUTE!'s Quick & Easy Guide to Excel on the Macintosh (131-5)	**$10.95**	_____
_____	COMPUTE!'s Quick & Easy Guide to Microsoft Word on the Macintosh (135-8)	**$10.95**	_____
_____	COMPUTE!'s Quick & Easy Guide to R:Base System V (132-2)	**$12.95**	_____
_____	COMPUTE!'s Quick & Easy Guide to OS/2 (137-4)	**$12.95**	_____
_____	COMPUTE!'s Quick & Easy Guide to Lotus 1-2-3 Macros (141-2)	**$10.95**	_____
_____	COMPUTE!'s Quick & Easy Guide to PC Excel (140-4)	**$10.95**	_____
_____	COMPUTE!'s Quick & Easy Guide to HyperCard (145-5)	**$12.95**	_____

*Add $2.00 per book for shipping and handling.
Outside US add $5.00 air mail or $2.00 surface mail.

NC residents add 5% sales tax _____
NY residents add 8.25% sales tax _____
Shipping & handling: $2.00/book _____
Total payment _____

All orders must be prepaid (check, charge, or money order).
All payments must be in US funds.
☐ Payment enclosed.
Charge ☐ Visa ☐ MasterCard ☐ American Express

Acct. No._____ Exp. Date _____
                                                                (Required)
Name _____

Address _____

City_____ State _____ Zip _____
*Allow 4–5 weeks for delivery.
Prices and availability subject to change.
Current catalog available upon request.